This is My Body

- and -

How Can I Pray?

by

Ian Petit OSB

New Life Publishing, Luton, UK

This edition published in 2004 by
New Life Publishing
15 Barking Close
Luton, LU4 9HG, UK

This is My Body first published in1991
by Darton Longman & Todd and reprinted in
1991, 1992, 1999 and 2000
How Can I Pray? first published in 1991
by Darton Longman & Todd and reprinted in
1993, 1996 and1999

ISBN 1 903623 16 2

Unless otherwise stated the biblical references in this
book are taken from The Jerusalem Bible, published and
copyright 1966, 1967 and 1968 by Darton, Longman
& Todd Ltd and Doubleday & Co. Inc.

British library Cataloguing in Publication Data.
A catalogue record for this book is available
from the British Library

Cover design by Yvonne Bell, www.vestments.co.uk.
Yvonne creates stoles, chasubles and copes
to individual design, often on silk.

New Life Publishing, Luton UK

Contents

This is my Body

How Can I Pray?

Acknowledgements

The Scripture quotations in this publication are based on *The Jerusalem Bible* published and copyright 1966, 1967 and 1968 by Darton, Longman and Todd Ltd and Doubleday and Co. Inc. Excerpts from the English translation of *The Roman Missal* are copyright 1973, International Committee on English in the Liturgy, Inc. All rights reserved.

Preface

The burst of glory that takes place, when the body and blood of the Lord are made present on the altar, cannot be known by the senses, nor can it be grasped by the mind. What has happened is so beyond the human realm of experience or understanding, that it can only be accepted on the authority of God. It is by faith that we accept our Lord's stark words, 'This is my body – this is my blood'. Once we start trying to understand how this can be, we get lost in endless human speculation. It is true, it can be argued that perhaps the Lord did not mean us to take his words literally, as when he talked about cutting off our right hand when it scandalizes us; but there are enough texts about eating and drinking his body and blood to suggest that he meant what he said.

Faith is beyond reason, not opposed to it. Our senses and our minds remain untouched; but faith tells us that we stand before the most important event in the history of the world. We stand present before the mystery of Christ; we are made present to the One who died for our sins and rose to new life so that we might live in a new way. All the hosts of heaven are prostrate around us, worshipping before this mystery where the One who is died for those who once were not. In the midst of this company we stand blind in our senses, uncomprehending in our minds. If we could but grasp the holiness of the moment made present to us, we, too, would lie face down calling out, 'Holy, holy is the Lord God of hosts'.

The Mass, though, has become very familiar to us, and I am reminded of a conversation I once had with a Hindu who was playing the part of Christ in a Mystery play. He came to attend Mass, and afterwards he remarked, 'But, how can you say it so quickly?' Actually that Mass had been rather reflective and slow, but I learnt much from his observation. He had found a profound sense of awe in playing the role of Christ in a play, and I began to reflect that if we really believe what is happening at Mass, why have many of us allowed it to become so familiar?

I fear we were introduced to the sign before comprehending the awesomeness of the reality behind that sign. This has certainly been true of me. From an early age, I believed the Mass to be important. I learnt how to follow it in my missal, and felt a certain pleasure in being able to be on the right page at the right time – but this did not bring the Mass alive for me.

It was only late in my life that I began to understand that 'to live' the gospel did not mean 'to practise the gospel precepts', but it meant to accept what Christ had done for me through his death and resurrection and be transformed by that truth. This gave me new life, this enabled me to live in a new way. Once I began to grasp the truth, I began to see that the Mass was the 're-presenting' of the saving event to us so that its mighty power may continue to affect us.

Much could be written on the Mass, and I have neither desire nor capability to write an exhaustive treatise or a history on it. I have wanted to share some insights and thoughts that I have had over the years in the hope that the Holy Spirit will breathe light into truths both old and new. I pray that as you read these pages and as you ponder the meaning of the Mass you will sense something of that burst of glory that envelops the whole of the worshipping family, drawing us all into the very holiness of God himself.

1

The Reality Behind the Sign

The spirit world cannot be felt, sensed or pictured. In it there is no space, no size, no colour. It is beyond our mind, beyond our grasp, beyond our senses.

A spiritual person is one who acknowledges that such a world exists. There are no convincing arguments for or against it; it is as though a decision is made, for some good reason, to believe or not to believe.

There is a knowing that does not come from proof, a certainty that does not result from arguments. Today, after a period when the spiritual world has been denied, there is a rediscovery of the spiritual dimension. This book deals with spiritual truth.

My Experience of the Mass

From my earliest days, I was told that the Mass was important, and because I trusted my parents and elders, I accepted what they said as true. I did not find very much satisfaction in it personally, but I had been told it was important, so it was important to me. I knew, in some way, it represented Calvary, but I found it hard to connect what I saw happening on the altar with what I knew happened outside the walls of Jerusalem. I also believed that Jesus came to me at the time of communion, and that, of course, meant a great deal.

My schooling days coincided with a time when it was thought good and proper for students to attend daily Mass. I cannot recall ever resenting that, even though I did not seem to draw much from it. It was something good Catholics did and I really did not give it all that much thought.

Such daily attendance of Mass by schoolchildren may seem surprising, but we need to remember that the scene then was very different from what it is today. Then, the Roman Catholic Church sought to keep a society of its own, subsisting in another society which was either Christian or non-Christian. Today, things have changed. In the western world there are many who are no longer Christian, and the Catholic Church, instead of trying to keep a closed society, is opening dialogue with modern-day thought. This has dismantled many of the bulwarks that protected the faithful, and it calls for the ordinary Catholic to be much more discerning and responsible.

The general upheaval has caused many new and

interesting ideas to be accessible to ordinary Catholics; and while this is good for it brings us out of the ghetto mentality by which we can be so protected that we jog along living on secondhand truths, it can also be harmful if we do not have a good, solid understanding of the basic Christian message as a foundation to our lives.

All this has produced considerable confusion and I see a need for solid teaching, especially with regard to fundamental gospel truths. As a priest, I meet today many who are literally lost because of all that has happened in the Church over these last thirty years. I think they are lost because the foundation truths were never securely laid. All too often we presume that these truths have been firmly grasped, when in fact that is far from the case.

We can be quite secure in belonging to a closed society, but when that society ceases to be closed, we can have a sense of being rudderless. All sorts of options now seem available, and while that can be good for the wise and discerning, it can be very unhelpful for the lost and confused. Frequently, it seems to me, the Mass is a cause for worry. Once it was in Latin, and that made it mysterious, but now that it is in the vernacular, people complain that the mystery has disappeared. But the mystery of the Mass is not in the language, it is in the making present of the sacrifice of Jesus on Calvary. I find that many people have not been well trained in the Scriptures which tell about the saving work of Jesus. If the saving work of Jesus has not been firmly grasped, then the re-presenting of that work under signs, will only be seen as signs and they will lack their full content.

11

What Do We Mean by Sacraments?

Sacraments are not magic. They are God's way of making his Son's redeeming work available to everyone. I sometimes wonder if many of us were introduced to the sacraments, the signs, and somehow never reached the reality behind those signs. We can be over-sacramentalized, and by that I mean that the importance of the sign can overshadow the reality. We all learnt the significance of Baptism, Confession, Mass and Holy Communion – but did we understand how the saving work of Christ was being administered to us through these different sacraments? Were we approaching the sacrament or the reality? I am well aware of the problem of communicating these truths to children, but I know from my own experience I never really understood the sacramental system until far too late in life.

In the gospel story of the woman with the haemorrhage who approached Jesus from behind, intending to touch the hem of his garment and be healed without drawing notice to herself, we are taught that although many were touching the Lord, it was the woman who had faith who was healed. So it is with sacraments, they are not magic – we have to approach with faith in what Jesus has done. We may receive the sacrament legitimately, but we can limit its effect by our lack of faith.

On the other hand it needs to be pointed out that although the woman had faith she was not healed until she had touched the Lord. Sacraments are the moment when we touch the Lord so that his saving work, which has been already achieved, floods into us. This makes it very important for us to know and

12

understand the Lord's work of salvation and then rejoice that we can receive it into ourselves through the signs he has left us.

Salvation is not something that we achieve ourselves, it is something we allow God to achieve in us. God's way of achieving it is through the death and resurrection of his Son. By dying and rising, Christ has broken the power of sin over our lives and enabled us to live in a new way. We can now live 'in Christ', rather than in our own strength. This is God's way of salvation and when we accept his way, which is not easy for it means renouncing all self-glory, then, through faith and the sacraments, the great work of Christ can begin to affect us. We need a firm understanding of this central truth if we are going to appreciate the gift of the Mass.

Two Saving Events

There are two great saving events in Scripture, one belongs to the Old Testament – when Moses led the Hebrews out of Egypt; the other belongs to the New Testament – when Jesus died on Calvary.

In the Old Testament story, after God had delivered the Hebrews from bondage in Egypt, they were told never to forget what the Lord had done for them.

> The Lord has brought you into the land which he swore to your fathers Abraham, Isaac and Jacob that he would give you. . . Then take care you do not forget the Lord your God who brought you out of the land of Egypt, out of the house of

slavery . . . In times to come, when your son asks you, 'What is the meaning of the decrees and laws and customs that the Lord God has laid down for you?' you shall tell your son, 'Once we were Pharaoh's slaves in Egypt, and the Lord God brought us out of Egypt by his mighty hand. Before our eyes the Lord God worked great and terrible signs and wonders against Egypt, against Pharaoh and all his House. And he brought us out from there to lead us into the land he swore to our fathers he would give to us.'

Deut 6:10, 12, 20–23

Not only were they to remember, constantly call to mind and teach this great deliverance that God had wrought for them, they were, each year, to re-enact what had happened. They were not to go through the same deliverance, but they were to call it to mind by ritual. They were to gather in families, dress as though they were going on a journey, slay an unblemished lamb and eat a meal similar to the one they were ordered to eat before the Exodus began. In this way they would bring the event so vividly to mind, that it would affect them afresh. This would keep their gratitude ever present and alive, and so they would not forget the goodness of God.

It was God who initiated the journey. The Hebrews did not decide to embark upon it. It was not planned, it was not a journey for gaining self-reliance, self-improvement – it was a journey decided upon by God, whereby he would transform his stiff-necked people. He would make them into a people who would trust him no matter what. In the desert all support was taken from them; they were faced with either perishing or trusting in God! God was forming his people in a rough school, so that when they entered the Promised Land, they would still trust in him and not in their new found wealth. Hence, in the Promised Land, there was an absolute need to remind themselves of what God had done for them, and to remind themselves forcibly, so that they might trust God rather than their arms, wealth or abundance.

In the New Testament Jesus said, 'Do this in memory of me' (Luke 22:19). He had just turned wine into his blood and bread into his body, demonstrating what was to happen on Calvary – his body and blood would be separated causing death. In the Mass, we make both Jesus' body and blood present, and thus we make his saving event present to us. We do not repeat it, we make ourselves present to this eternal happening. In other words, we call to mind the New Testament's saving event, just as the Hebrews called to mind their saving event – the Exodus from Egypt. We do this for many reasons; one is that we will never forget it, another is that its saving power will still be applied to us.

Of all the events of the New Testament, the most central and important is that Jesus took our sins upon himself on Calvary and paid the penalty by dying. The death that he entered was unable to hold this innocent One, so the Father called his beloved, obedient Son back out of death. Jesus did not come back to life in the same way that Lazarus did; Lazarus was resuscitated, Jesus rose to new life. He did not return to what he had been before. He was new, yet different, the same Jesus but alive in a new way. Here was the One from whom the new race of humans would spring, and anyone who now believes in him can share in this new life. This is the great truth that we call to mind at every Mass and celebrate with prayers of wonder and thanksgiving. I will return to this truth many times in the course of this book.

From the earliest of times the Church has gathered together to fulfil the Lord's command – 'Do this in memory of me'. Our earliest record of this comes from Justin the Martyr. He wrote around AD 150, and described how people would come from different areas to gather in one place. There they would listen to readings either from the apostles or one of the prophets. This was followed by a short address given by the one presiding. Prayers were said, then bread and wine were brought and presented; the president gave thanks and all said 'Amen'. Then the eucharistic gifts were distributed, and the deacons were sent to bring them to those who could not be present.

Today we follow the same pattern – there are prayers and readings, bread and wine are offered, we give thanks to God and do what the Lord told us to do – we break bread and say the very words he said and make his body present to us; we do the same with the wine making his blood present, thus symbolizing his death whereby his body and blood were separated. The death and rising of Christ is the very means by which God has rescued us, and we celebrate its truth and ponder its deep meaning as it becomes present to us. We will never ponder its full significance, and so time and again we come before this mystery and allow ourselves to be caught up in its power and healing. Over the centuries the prayers and readings have become set, not in a static sense, but rather because over the years, in well chosen words, they have distilled the deep meaning of God's love for us.

Having made ourselves present to the saving work of Christ, we then do what Christ commanded us to do – we eat his body and drink his blood. 'For my flesh is real food and my blood is real drink. He who eats my flesh and drinks my blood lives in me and I live in him' (Jn 6:56). A Christian is someone who lives in Christ and allows Christ to live in him. There is a difference between 'having' life and 'living' life. It is one thing to have Christ 'in' us, another to allow him 'to live in' us.

The saving work of Christ has been completed. Jesus' last words were, 'It is finished' (Jn 19:30). Yet this work has not been completed as far as we are concerned, and not yet begun for those still to be born. This is the task of the Holy Spirit – to reveal who Christ is and what he has done for us by his death and resurrection; and as we accept these truths in an ever deeper way, the Spirit causes the work of Jesus to affect us more radically. In the Eucharist we have the very central work of Christ, his death and resurrection, made present to us, and we are given the extraordinary privilege of being exposed to this saving event, offering it in thanksgiving to the Father and then receiving as food and drink the very body and blood of the Lord so that his life in us may be strong and active.

Again this is not to make us holy in the sense that we accumulate holy virtues, holy ways of doing things, as though we become holy in ourselves. God alone is holy, and we are holy only in so far as we are in him. God's plan is not that we set out on 'virtue gathering courses', but that we allow him to transform us into the image of his Son. As the Hebrews were called to make a journey that they did not plan or even want, so, too, we will be led, as Peter, where we would rather not go. God has a plan for our life, our work is to allow him his way. 'Come follow me' – the way he went was a way of self-giving, a pouring out, a losing, a wasting. 'Do this in memory of me.'

2

You Gather a People to Yourself

 There is so much more to being a Christian than our personal salvation. When we become Christians we enter a family, we join a body, we become members of the Church. This is not the same as being a member of a club; we are actually grafted onto the body of Christ, and become living members, sharing in his life with all the other members. Just as any part of the human body needs to remain in the body if it is to stay alive, so, too, a Christian is committed to unity with the other members.

We do not go to Mass because we feel like going. We go because we are called. God calls us to come together as the body of his Son and offer to the Father the most perfect offering that could be made, the very offering of Christ himself. We do not choose the members of our natural family, so neither do we choose the members of the Church. In a parish we are given our brothers and sisters in

Christ. All the faithful have a right to be there and we are all equal before the Lord. Earthly differences are of no consequence.

Now that the Mass is in the vernacular, and there are 'folk' and 'traditional' Masses, there can be a tendency to go shopping for one that suits our taste. While this is understandable, it does cut at the sense of parish being the local body of Christ. The Mass is the Mass no matter what form it takes. There may be a need for a parish to consider carefully whether its form of Mass is the most helpful, but it is sad when a parish divides and people end up by going to this church or that and have no commitment to the other members who worship with them. We are called to be a people who are alive with the life of the Risen Lord; we do not just happen to use the same building; we are not like people who use the same restaurant.

Introduction to the Mass

The Mass begins with a simple preparation. The first thing we do is to make the sign of the Cross. By this gesture we remind ourselves of the three Persons of the Trinity, calling to mind the Father who so loved the world that he sent his Son; the Son who out of love for the Father and the world came to bear the sins of the world, and thus save the world; and the Holy Spirit who continuously is coming to us to make effective in us the plan of the Father made possible by the Son's obedience.

The priest then greets the people who have gathered together from many different parts, thus forming the body of Christ, so that they can offer the

Father worthy praise and worship. Many talents and gifts will be required to make this gathering fruitful. There will be readers, who are to proclaim the Word of God. Reading at Mass involves much more than reading the Word of God aloud. The Word of God is something alive, and if we just read it as a piece of reading, then we may well prevent the message from reaching the people gathered there. I believe it is important for the congregation to pray that the reader be anointed by the Spirit of God, so that hearts may be moved. The readers, in their turn, need to appreciate the solemn privilege of being the mouthpiece for God's Word.

There will also be those who enrich the service with their singing, and again how important it is to see that this is not a performance; in some way the singing must bring people actually to worship God. Then there will be those who serve, those who take collections, those who welcome people, those who assist with the children of the parish. There are many duties to perform to help this body come before the Lord. The priest's solemn role is to bring the Holy Spirit down on our own gifts, transforming them into the sacrifice of Christ, and together with the people to offer that to the Father.

All these different roles show that we form together the body of Christ, we are not individuals on individual journeys, we belong to each other, we share a new life together. Because we fail to live this extraordinary truth, we are invited at the beginning of the Mass to confess our sins to God and one another.

I was once present at a Mass in Rome where a Central American bishop was the main celebrant.

He reminded us of how easy it is to give responses by rote without much thought for the meaning behind them. For example, it is so easy to reply to the invitation, 'Lift up your hearts', with, 'We've lifted them up to the Lord', and yet have our hearts anything but lifted up. He then suggested that we had an opportunity now to mean what we were going to say. He told us that we were about to say, 'I confess to Almighty God, and to you, my brothers and sisters, that I have sinned'. 'Would you please turn to the brother or sister on your left and right, and confess a sin,' were his next words. You can imagine the panic that broke out. If I had known that this was going to happen, I would have made sure where I stood and who would be next to me. The result actually was very moving. Having dared to say something to our neighbour, and it did not have to be anything very startling, we all sensed our common need for God's forgiveness. This united us and we went into that eucharistic celebration sensing very much our oneness, and when we asked for God's mercy our prayer was heartfelt.

On feast days the 'Gloria' is said or sung – a beautiful prayer which celebrates the sheer goodness of God. We thank him for being who he is. We bless him, we honour him, we worship him. Here is prayer which is all God-ward. Petition is present, but we do not focus on it, rather our sense of God's great glory makes us aware of our shallowness and so we call out to him to 'hear our prayer'. In our own private prayers it can be helpful to create our own 'gloria' and to think of all the reasons we have for praising God.

Following the reconciliation, and the 'Gloria' if

there is one, the priest leads us in a prayer, a prayer that is shaped by and takes into account the liturgical season that we are in. For example, during Advent we focus on the Lord's coming, so the prayer during that season talks of the different 'comings' of Jesus. He has come in history, he needs to come continually to us in a personal way, and there is his final coming in glory. We use this season to remind ourselves how much the Chosen People longed for his coming, and to stir ourselves also to long with ardour for the Lord.

During Lent the flavour of the prayer is repentance and sorrow for sin, and as we approach Holy Week we reflect on the mystery of the suffering and death of Christ. All this helps us to appreciate the Father's wondrous plan for our salvation.

I was once saying Mass in the USA, and when I said to the people, 'Let us pray,' to my astonishment they all burst into vocal prayer. Then I realized that I had invited them to pray. This helped me to understand why the prayer said at that time in the Mass is called the 'collect' – the priest's prayer collects the prayers of the people together.

This introductory part to the Mass is a simple preparation for entering into the Mass proper, where we start by listening to God's Word.

3

Speak, Lord, Your Servant is Listening

 The basic format for the Mass has remained virtually unchanged over the centuries. There are readings taken from the Word of God, readings which link the Mass to the synagogue gatherings, and then comes the breaking of bread, introducing the Lord's gift to his Church.

In the early days the readings were not arranged as they are today. Then the reader simply read as long as there was time or it seemed appropriate. Today, on Sundays or feast days, there are three readings and these are chosen to fit in with the liturgical season. The first reading is normally taken from the Old Testament, but this is replaced by one from the Acts of the Apostles during Paschal time. The second reading comes from one of the letters of the New Testament. The third reading is a gospel passage. During Advent, Christmas, Lent and Paschal time all three readings are linked; but in ordinary time this is only true of the first reading and the gospel. The second reading then works through one of the epistles giving appropriate sections each Sunday.

Jews gathered in the synagogue primarily to hear God's law proclaimed, and to learn about this God who had adopted the Jews as his chosen people and had worked such marvels for their deliverance.

The Jewish people had a great reverence for the Word of God. The Word of God, spoken and then written down on stone tablets or scrolls, was God's presence among them. The early Christians wanted to keep this reading aloud of Scripture because it was important for knowing God and learning the plan he had for his people; and, besides, it helped keep a link between the Jewish custom and the development of Christianity. It was also a very fitting preparation for the breaking of bread.

In some Protestant churches you will not see the altar in the centre but rather a pulpit with the book of Scriptures enshrined upon it. In many Catholic churches the tabernacle is in the centre with the altar, though since Vatican II there has been a return to the practice whereby the Blessed Sacrament is reserved in a side chapel, leaving the altar of sacrifice in the middle. Also since Vatican II the book of Scriptures is enthroned in the sanctuary. At solemn Masses it is carried in at the beginning, held high, and, before the reading, carried in procession with reverence and dignity. The changes since Vatican II are not radical innovations, rather they are a return to how things once were. God comes to us and is present in both Word and Sacrament.

The Word liturgy is an important part of the Mass for through it we allow God to speak to us so that we might respond to him. We Catholics have not been well grounded in our Scriptures, and we need to take advantage of the books and courses now available to help us understand God's Word. We are not all asked to be scholars, but we are called to listen to God's Word and be formed by it as we obey it.

Old Testament

The books of the Old Testament can be quite a stumbling block because God can appear a bit temperamental, at times very angry and causing terrible catastrophes, then repenting and promising all sorts of blessings to his people. It is important, though, to remember that the authors are describing God as they perceived him, and not as he really is. No idea that we have of God, is God. Our ideas of him are very limited and over the years they change. All of us have thought of God in different ways, at some times we have imagined him benign, at others, cruel, distant, near, loving or frightening. Life is a pilgrimage – a getting to know God. Older people may smile when they remember some of the ways they used to think about God. Time and experience have caused them to change their ideas.

This is why it is important to listen to the Word of God over and over again, for as we change, so we hear the Word differently. The Word, by itself, will not always change us because we can develop a set frame of mind whereby we prevent the Word entering in to transform us. This is where we need the touch of the Lord through the sacraments, setting us free to hear his Word. In the Mass we cele-

31

brate both the Word touching us through Scripture and touching us through sacrament.

The Chosen People had to grow in their under-standing of God. To start off with they had simple and uncomplicated ideas. They understood that God was good and wanted them to be good also, and naturally they concluded that if they were good then God would bless them. God had to lead them beyond this tit for tat relationship; he had to reveal to them that there was more to life than prosperous farms and large families. They were in danger of viewing their relationship with him in very selfish terms. All this could develop into a selfish friend-ship. Slowly they began to see that good people could also suffer and evil people prosper. As they wrestled with these difficulties, men were inspired to write about them.

The book of Job, for example, attempts to explain why the good suffer. Satan had complained to God that no wonder Job was such a God-fearing person, he had every blessing he could have wished for. Satan asked permission to strike at his possessions, and when that did not make Job curse God, he attacked his person. The story is fiction, but it has truths to teach. Job's friends all come and argue that he must have sinned against God. Job contends that he is innocent, but towards the end of the book he complains that God has been a bit hard on him. Job is ticked off by God for questioning him, and the story ends with Job being reinstated with even more blessings and wealth. It does not answer the prob-lem of suffering, but it wrestles with it.

Sections from different books of the Old Testa-ment are drawn upon according to the liturgical season. Isaiah features a great deal during Advent with his more apocalyptical passages being used to direct our gaze towards the Lord who has come and who is still to come. During Lent readings are taken from a variety of books illustrating the unfaithfulness of God's people and their need for repentance. All this is to direct our thoughts to our own relationship with God.

Psalms

After the first reading there is the responsorial psalm. Here the Church asks us to respond to the first reading by putting a psalm on our lips. You will notice that this psalm is connected to the reading we have just heard. It is not just any old psalm chosen at random. It responds to the message of the first reading. In doing this the Church is teaching us to respond, not just with our lips, but also with our hearts. This is why we need to listen to what we are saying or singing, and not give responses parrot-fashion.

New Testament

The epistles and the gospels tell us what God has done for us through the life, death and resurrection of Jesus – that through Christ's death and resurrection, sin has been forgiven and a new life has begun, a life which we draw from Christ. We need to keep this thought in our minds while we listen to these readings.

Not every reading we listen to will talk specifically of the death and resurrection of Christ. With regard to the gospels, more often than not we listen to accounts of the miracles of Christ or some teaching that he gave. But unless our minds have the central message of the gospel clearly fixed in them, we will listen to the readings and miss the point of what we are hearing. We may well admire the story, be moved with wonder at his power and concern, but never connect that this same Jesus is alive today, and therefore can minister to us as well. He who gave new sight to the blind, can give us, who are so spiritually blind, new sight to see the truth. Too often we imagine these gifts are for the 'holy', the 'good'.

So, when we read the gospels we are not just looking back to the time of Christ and seeing what he did at that time as though we were reading a bit of history. Nor are we being told, 'This is how to live, now you get on with it'. Rather we are reminding ourselves that this same Jesus is alive and working amongst us today, and that he wants us to live in his strength, not our own. If, for example, the day's reading focuses on Jesus' teaching about love of our neighbour, we could listen to it, and then go off and try to put it into practice, and get thoroughly frustrated by our inability to love. This could lead to discouragement or feelings of guilt and failure. It would hardly be good news, and we might be tempted to give up on Christianity if it seemed to bring nothing but struggle and frustration. But the gospel message is not meant to send us off trying to fulfil its teachings in our own power, it is seeking to show us who Jesus is and that it is only in him that we can be fruitful. This is why we must listen to the gospel reading, knowing in our hearts the basic message.

The epistles, especially St Paul's, are more complex. Often the authors are writing about situations which we, unless we are historians, do not understand. They are dealing with problems that have arisen in the early Christian communities, and reading these letters without too much background can be confusing. As the apostles spread the news of Jesus, they kept in touch with the cities where they had made converts. The letters they wrote are known as the epistles. In these letters we see the 'Church' trying to explain the teachings about Jesus Christ. They are a fund of deep insights into the mystery of Christ. A number are written by men who knew the Lord both before and after his resurrection and were present when the Holy Spirit came down with such power and might. Again the good news of Jesus Christ is being spelled out to us showing how it is a development, and not a contradiction, of the Jewish teachings. Again the message is that through Christ's death and resurrection, sin has been forgiven and a new life has been given to enable us to live in a new way.

Paul claimed to have learnt his understanding of Christ through a revelation and not from the other apostles. The great theme, which he deals with, is that observance of the law does not save us. We are saved by belief in Jesus Christ. The Jews had been brought up to live a life dependent on God. This life of dependence on God was illustrated by the kind of life that the law laid down. The law said, 'A man of God will live like this'. It is easy to see how this changed into, 'If I live that sort of life, then I must be a man of God'.

Fallen man is unable to live such a life, so the law of God became, not a means of being set free, but a proof that mankind is not free. It showed man's need of healing. God, in the prophet Ezekiel, promised man a new heart and God's own spirit. Jesus is the new man with the new heart and God's own spirit. The New Testament calls us to believe in Jesus Christ and receive a new heart and spirit from him.

These basic truths are of utmost importance because they help us listen to the Word of God with some understanding of God's plans for the human race. Because for much of my life my ideas of God had been very faulty, I found the Word confusing, obscure and irrelevant. It just did not touch me, or it made me feel fearful and very inadequate. After some considerable time I slowly came to realize that God is on my side, that he loves me and has sent his Son that I might live a new life in him. Only as I began to grasp the real message of the gospel did I find the Word helpful and full of meaning.

Our Response to the Word

We will all hear the Word of God as individuals. God speaks to each of us where we are. That is why it can be so fruitful when we share what each of us has heard. The Word of God can correct us, encourage us, enlighten us. It is not meant to fill us with despair.

Having listened to the Word, we are now ready to enter into the action of the Mass. The readings will have shown us our need of God; either we will want to thank him and dedicate our lives to him, or we will want to say sorry and ask him to change us, or we will just want to place ourselves in his safe-keeping. All this fits us for the next main stage in the Mass where we will offer ourselves to God under the signs of bread and wine.

Homily

On Sundays, after the gospel, the priest gives a homily. A homily is not a sermon, a homily gives light to the readings. It is meant to help the people grasp the message of what has been read. It is important that the congregation pray for the priest and ask that he will truly break the Word of God for them, that he will put the readings in context and show what is being said to them today. At the end of the homily every one stands to declare their faith in the triune God.

4

We Believe

We can easily imagine that saying something by rote is the same as saying it by heart. But to say something by rote means saying the words without thought to their meaning, whereas to say something by heart means assenting with our hearts to what we say with our lips.

When we say the Creed, or any prayer for that matter, it is important that we listen to what we say, so as to allow our hearts to assent. In the Creed we list our beliefs in God and his actions.

'We believe in one God.' As a body we state our belief. We are not a lot of individuals proclaiming our personal faith; we state that we, as one body, believe in one God. None of us causes our own existence, it is God who calls us into being, therefore we all share a common origin. God is the One who is, we are the ones who once were not. We share this common ground with all creation. Our value is not because of what we do, our value is because the One who makes us does not make mistakes.

God is not just our creator, he is our Father because of our union with Christ Jesus, and we affirm him as Father and Almighty. He is not our Father by nature, but by adoption; that is, he has chosen us to be his children and given us new life as children of God.

We also affirm our belief in the Son of God, who springs eternally from the Father. The Son is not the Father, yet he is co-equal to the Father. This is a deep mystery, which our minds, confined to think within the limits of time and space, cannot grasp. We also state our belief that the Son was involved in the creation of all things. The Father spoke his Word and things happened. The Word of God is his Son, hence 'through him all things were made'.

All these affirmations refer to the mysterious relationship between the Father and the Son. We then confess our belief in God's plan for us creatures wounded by sin. We acknowledge that God so loved the world that he sent his only Son into this world to save it. We accept the extraordinary truth that through the power of the Holy Spirit God's Son took flesh in the womb of a virgin and became one of the human family. Jesus did this so that he might repair the damage incurred by the human race when it sinned against God. By choosing to live off the tree of knowledge of good and evil rather than the tree of life, Adam rejected God's plan for the human race. The tree of life represents the indwelling of the Holy Spirit, and when man rejected this guidance, it meant the human race could no longer know God intimately. Jesus came to repair this damage by dying on the cross and because he was God this act of his would have infinite value and could cancel any debt; and because he was man, he stood for the human family, bearing our sin and cancelling our debt.

What extraordinary truths are summed up in these very matter-of-fact statements. We express our belief that God so loved the world that he sent his only Son into it knowing that we would bruise him and cast him out of the city and watch him die. There is no word painting in these statements; they are a clear and direct declaration of our faith and we need to be sure that we do actually believe them.

Once Jesus had died the kingdom of death could not keep him captive for he was innocent, and so the Father called him to rise to new life through the power of the Holy Spirit. For the Christian everything centres round the fact that the Lord died and rose to new life, thus conquering death. Death is for the sinner, Jesus was innocent and so death could not keep hold of him. Because of his rising we have a certainty, that united to him, we, too, will die and rise to everlasting life.

We assert our belief that he is coming again to complete the kingdom that is already among us and to judge the living and the dead. We declare our faith and belief in the third Person, the Holy Spirit, who proceeds from the Father and the Son. The Father puts the whole of himself into the love he has for the Son; the Son puts the whole of himself into the love he has for the Father; the love between them is the Holy Spirit, a Person – God.

We accept that Jesus founded a universal Church through which the Spirit of God continues to make effective all that Jesus did by dying for the forgive-

ness of sins and rising that we might have eternal
life.

Having stated our faith in the fundamental essen-
tials of the Christian faith we now proceed to offer
the sacrifice of praise to God.

5

Through Your Goodness We Have This Bread to Offer

The word 'sacrifice' denotes for most of us something painful, difficult, costly. We think of surrendering, giving up a precious possession. The word actually comes from two Latin words, 'sacrum facere', meaning 'to make holy'. The idea behind this was to take something you held precious and put it into the safe-keeping of a god. This, clearly, meant being separated from your possession, but the object of the exercise was not so much the being separated from the possession as the putting it into the safe-keeping of a deity.

However, this basic idea of sacrifice became overshadowed by all sorts of other motives, and instead of asking for the safe protection of the object, the object became a gift to the deity for some favour in return. Thus the modern word now has the meaning of 'surrendering', 'giving up', and we do not think of 'making holy'. It is important for us to grasp the original and true meaning, and to realize that sacrificing something need not be a painful process. We can compare it to giving someone a present. Imagine giving the present and then bursting into tears because we have been separated from our gift. This would be to miss the whole object of giving the present – it was not to cause us pain but to give pleasure to the other, even if it means losing our gift.

At the Offertory in the Mass, we offer bread and wine. God does not need bread and wine, he is the Lord of the universe and he has no need of our gifts. What we are actually offering is ourselves, under the signs of bread and wine. These are good representatives because we all need food and drink to live. After hearing the Word of God in the readings for the day, we should all be ready to surrender ourselves, either in gratitude for his goodness or in repentance for our failures. In some way we want to put ourselves into God's safe-keeping.

We cannot all go up to the altar and give ourselves there and then to God, so we send up something to represent us. In some churches, as we enter there is a basket with hosts in it and beside it there is a silver bowl, and if we are going to go to Holy Communion, we place a host in the bowl. During the Offertory that bowl is brought up to the altar with the wine and water. While that is happening we should unite ourselves to the action by deliberately thinking of our gift of self to God. Also when the priest is offering the bread and wine, we should remember that we, too, are making that offering with him. Therefore if a hymn is to be sung at that moment, it should be a hymn which identifies with the action, so that we are not distracted from what we are doing. To sing a hymn to Mary or one of the saints would be to distract us from the action we are all involved in.

After the wine has been poured into the chalice and before it is offered, a drop of water is added to it. The prayer said at that moment indicates the meaning of this action. 'By the mystery of this water and wine may we come to share in the divinity of Christ, who humbled himself to share in our humanity' – the wine representing Christ's divinity and the water our humanity. Here we have summed up the mystery of God's plan for us. He calls us to be united with his Son. His Son became a member of the human race and was the first of that race to live, by his own power, without sin. When he died he became the sacrificial Lamb, taking the sins of the world upon himself and gaining forgiveness for them, and because he was God that action was able to cancel all sin. To stop us continuing in sin he offers to live in all those who accept what he has done.

There is absolutely nothing we can do to unite ourselves to Christ. We could not make ourselves worthy of such a thing. All we can do is to offer ourselves to God and invite him to come and unite us to his Son. The saving work of Christ has been completed – 'It is accomplished' – but it is not yet accomplished in us and in all those yet to be born. This is what Church is about, it is the family through which the saving work of Christ may be administered to the generations that succeed him. That is why it is so important to understand what is happening at the Mass. We are offering ourselves so that God will take us into his safe-keeping by uniting us to his Son and the offering he made of himself.

At one time people used to bring all sorts of gifts to the church, and at the Offertory these were brought up to the altar with the bread and wine. These gifts were to be distributed to the poor and needy. I saw this revived when I was studying French in Paris. At St Sevrin, a parish on the left bank, all sorts of goods were brought up at the Offertory. I then realized why the priest washes his hands after the offering of the bread and wine. At one time he would have collected raw vegetables and he would need cleaning up before going on with the Mass. The washing is now spiritualized, and as he washes his hands he asks for cleansing from sin.

Pagan and Old Testament Sacrifices

There are three main phases to a sacrifice: there is the offering of the gift or gifts; then comes the acceptance of the offering, the making it holy; and finally there is the communion with the gift that has been made holy. The actions surrounding a sacrifice are symbolic. In pagan sacrifices, and in the Old Testament, the gods or God did not come and take hold of what was offered, so some sign was shown to indicate that the gift had now passed into the possession of the deity. If the gift was an animal then its life was taken, and to ensure the carcass was not kept for food it was destroyed by fire. Here the gift was utterly taken out of the offerers' keeping. Sometimes it was the first fruits of the field that were offered, again these were often burnt as a sign of the gift being taken totally away. Primitive people thought that God or the gods needed these gifts, but soon the Chosen People began to see that the gifts they offered God stood for themselves. They were not allowed to take their own life, so they took something precious to themselves and let that gift represent themselves. By taking the life of the animal they were showing that they did not consider themselves worthy of their gift of life, and they offered the life of the animal in place of their own to make amends for sin.

In the Mass we, too, offer our life to God; we have sinned and we declare that death is our punishment and we want to put our life into the safekeeping of God. God takes our offering and makes it holy by changing it into the very offering that his Son made by giving his own life for the ransom of many. In the following chapter we will examine this extraordinary truth. But before we look into this mystery, we need to understand that at the Offertory we are asking God to accept our life and all its mistakes. The offering we make is not just bread and wine, we take these symbols and offer in reality our very self. And so the priest ends this part of the Mass by saying: 'Pray, brothers and sisters, that my sacrifice and yours may be acceptable to God, the almighty Father.'

6

Let Us Give Thanks to the Lord Our God

Having gathered together and asked pardon of God and one another; having listened to the Word of God and been brought again to that place where we want to surrender to him; and having offered ourselves to him under the signs of bread and wine – we now enter into the Eucharistic Prayer, the prayer by which we make present to ourselves God's great saving act of the death and resurrection of Jesus Christ.

This tremendous thanksgiving prayer begins with the prefaces. These are a variety of prayers used during different seasons and on different feast days. They are masterpieces, for they sum up profound truths in simple phrases. In some ways they sound too simple and we can easily slide over them and fail to see the fullness of their meaning. Because they are seasonal they emphasize the truth of the feast we celebrate.

During this chapter I will quote from the prefaces to indicate how they teach us the mysteries that

God has revealed to us. In these prayers the Church shows us what God has done for us and leads us to praise and worship him for his great power and love.

In the first week of Lent, we pray to the Father:

As we recall the great events that gave us new
    life in Christ,
you bring the image of your Son to perfection
    within us.

Here is a clear teaching on what holiness means and how we allow it to happen within us. It clearly is not something that we achieve, it is something that God achieves in us, and we open ourselves to it by calling to mind all that God has done for us in Christ Jesus. It is believing in the saving work of Christ that opens us to its healing power. Holiness is to have the image of the Son brought to perfection within us.

If we are to recall these great saving events we need to know what they are. God sent his only Son to bear the consequences of our sins. Death is the penalty for sin and so the Son of God came to die in our place. Before he could die for us he had to have a life that was capable of dying because as God he could not die. And so the Church teaches us in Christmas preface 3:

Your eternal Word has taken upon himself our
    human weakness,
giving our mortal nature immortal value.
So marvellous is this oneness between God and
    man

that in Christ man restores to man the gift of
everlasting life.

And from Christmas preface 1:

In the wonder of the incarnation
your eternal Word has brought to the eyes of
faith
a new and radiant vision of your glory.
In him we see our God made visible
and so are caught up in love of the God we
cannot see.

When God sent his Son he did not send him as
a new creation so that he could start the human
family afresh, he sent him to be born from one of
the daughters of Adam:

Through the power of the Holy Spirit,
she became the virgin mother of your only Son,
our Lord Jesus Christ,
who is for ever the light of the world.

Our Lady 1

God in his great mercy came to our rescue. We
were incapable of making sufficient reparation for
sin, so he sent his Son, who as God could make
worthy reparation, and since he came among us as
a man, he was able to be our legitimate representa-
tive.

We see your infinite power
in your loving plan of salvation.
You came to our rescue by your power as God,
but you wanted us to be saved by one like us.

57

Man refused your friendship,
but man himself was to restore it
through Jesus Christ our Lord.

Sundays 3

Christ sent his Son to be a second Adam, he came to undo what the first had done. Adam lost life through a tree, Christ comes to restore it by the tree of the Cross.

You decreed that man should be saved through
   the wood of the cross.
The tree of man's defeat became his tree of
   victory;
where life was lost, there life has been restored
   through Christ our Lord.

Triumph of the Cross

In these beautiful prayers we worship God by reminding ourselves of his plans and also we are instructed in what God has done for us, so that by constantly being reminded of his love and care we may enter deeper and deeper into, and thus open ourselves to receive in an ever fuller way, the richness of salvation.

Liturgy is not theatre – it is not acting out scenes from the past so that we may be spectators to them; it is remembering, through words and signs, moments when Jesus overcame evil, so that what happened at those moments can affect us here and now. This is made possible through the working of the Holy Spirit, who has been sent to reveal to us what Jesus has done, and when we accept what he has done the Spirit brings the work of Jesus to fruition in us here today.

Eucharistic Prayers

There are four main Eucharistic Prayers together with several for children and reconciliation services. All these recall, in different ways, the death, resurrection and ascension of the Lord. Here, again, we find these prayers so packed with truths that we can miss their richness.

It was only after I had come to understand the centrality of the Lord's death and resurrection that I began to appreciate the Mass. It is so easy to think of the gospel as a code for moral behaviour. After all there are many injunctions to be good, truthful, loving. This turns the gospel into Good Advice, and not Good News – for it is discouraging to learn how difficult it is always to be loving and forgiving. The good news of the gospel is that through our union with Christ we can live in a new way. Union with Christ is not won as a reward for good effort, it is given to those who confess their weakness and throw themselves on the mercy of God who sent his Son to be our saviour.

In these prayers of thanksgiving we address the Father by calling to mind all that he has done for us through the work of his Son. Calvary is not repeated in the Mass, for that is impossible to do, but it is re-presented – made present to us, so that it may continually affect us. By listening to and praying these beautiful prayers, we are taught the fundamental truths of our faith. More important than the great miracles that Jesus did, more important than his teaching on morality, is the fact that God sent his Son to redeem us. He allowed himself to be besmirched with our sins and suffer the consequences, and thus paid for our sins more than adequately. But that was not all – death could not keep hold of this innocent One, and in obedience to the Father he rose up from the dead, thus conquering death. Here was the new Adam and from him the new human race would spring. So how fitting it is that we begin our thanksgiving to this loving Father with the words:

> Father, you are holy indeed,
> and all creation rightly gives you praise.

This is the very reason the Church has gathered us together. We have come to give thanks and praise to God for his mighty deeds.

Then we state what he has done:

> All life, all holiness comes from you . . .

This is a clear expression of the truth that we do not make ourselves holy, and the prayer goes on to explain how holiness comes to us:

> through your Son, Jesus Christ Our Lord . . .

Jesus is the One who took our human nature and made it holy and transmitted that holiness to us:

> by the working of the Holy Spirit.

Here, in very simple phrases, is stated the heart of

60

the gospel, and as we pray these prayers we should be saying to ourselves, 'That is true. That is true'.

Next, we present our offering to God, the offering we made of ourselves under the form of bread and wine, and we ask God to make our gifts holy through the power of his Holy Spirit.

And so, Father, we bring you these gifts.
We ask you to make them holy by the power of your Spirit . . .

At this moment we again offer ourselves willingly to the Father. All our cares, worries and weaknesses we surrender into his hands.

The only way that the Spirit makes anything holy is by uniting it to the Holy One, Jesus Christ, and we humbly ask God to do this for us:

We ask you to make them holy by the power of your Spirit,
that they may become the body + and blood
of your Son, our Lord Jesus Christ,
at whose command we celebrate this eucharist.

As a priest, now standing facing the people, I find this a very moving moment. We have all offered ourselves under the signs of bread and wine, and now as I say over the bread the words, 'This is my body', I see the people in the background and I am saying over them, 'This is my body' – the gift of ourselves that we have offered has been made holy by being united to the Holy One, Christ. In other words we have been Christed. The Holy Spirit of God is uniting us to Christ at the very moment when he gave himself totally to the Father on Calvary. On Calvary, his body and blood were separated, causing death; on our altar, through the separate consecrations, his body and blood have been sacramentally separated, making Calvary sacramentally present, and we have been caught up into it very intimately. We now have the extraordinary privilege of offering to the Father the gift that his Son made of himself, with us caught up in that gift. The great prayer continues:

Father, calling to mind the death your Son
 endured for our salvation . . .

What thought can we possibly find to call to mind that which has just been made real in front of us? Jesus heaving desperately on the Cross trying to catch his breath. Pushing against the nails in his feet to relieve the restriction in his chest, then sagging again once the pain of the nails in his feet became too great. God dying for his creatures. In a sense he is apologizing to his suffering creatures, by taking on himself rejection, suffering, abandonment, yet never opening his mouth to complain or draw attention to himself and what he is doing for us. A deep silence, not a word from him save that which had to be said.

We have but a moment to call this to mind, but that moment can be full if we have spent many moments pondering long on the mystery that God chose to die in our place. We cannot make this mystery touch us in the depths of our being. We may be able to stir our emotions, but that will not last. We can but stand, waiting till the Holy Spirit makes us know what our minds cannot know. Once this has happened a very quick calling to mind can be extremely profound and full. But unless we have pondered long, our calling to mind will be perfunctory, or alas, it may be no more than words while our minds are busy with their own affairs.

In the eucharist we celebrate the whole saving event, not just the death of the Lord, but also his rising and going back to the Father. So the prayer continues, calling to mind:

> his glorious resurrection and ascension into
>   heaven,
> and ready to greet him when he comes again,
> we offer you in thanksgiving this holy and living
>   sacrifice.

What an extraordinary privilege it is to be able to offer to the Father the gift his Son made of himself. Note the prayer says 'we' offer you. The whole people offer this living sacrifice to the Father. What an incredible honour! This is what is meant by the priesthood of the laity: all who are in the body of Christ are able to offer Christ's death and resurrection to the Father – a living sacrifice of praise. The ordained priest makes this sacrifice present on the altar, but the whole body offers it to the Father.

We now ask the Father to look favourably on this offering:

> Look with favour on your Church's offering,
> and see the Victim whose death has reconciled
>   us to yourself.

Here we state the central truth that salvation is not due to us for anything that we have done, but it has been won for us by the death and resurrection of the Son of God. He has reconciled us to the Father.

> Grant that we, who are nourished by his body
> and blood,
> may be filled with his Holy Spirit,
> and become one body, one spirit in Christ.

Because we are not holy of ourselves, we ask that we may be united more and more intimately with the Holy One through the work of the Holy Spirit. It is the Spirit's task to sanctify. He does this by revealing to us the truth, and as we accept it, he unites us to the Holy One, Jesus Christ.

We next ask that we be made a gift to the Father and thus join the family that the Son has won for him.

> May he make us an everlasting gift to You . . .

What an incredible thought that is – we become the gift that the Son gives to his Father; a gift bought at a terrible cost. And so we ask all the saints to intercede constantly for us that we may never fail to see the truth of the mysteries that we are involved in. The depth of these truths is infinite, hence we need to return time and time again to their reality and allow their power to penetrate deeper and deeper.

Having pondered with wonder all that God has

done for us, the human family, we now ask that it may have effect in the world of today.

Lord, may this sacrifice
which has made our peace with you,
advance the peace and salvation of all the world.

We remember the Catholic family, and we ask God's blessing on the Pope and the bishops and then we ask God to 'unite all your children wherever they may be'. I love the universality of this prayer, showing as it does the Church's concern for everybody. We also pray for the departed and we first mention 'our departed brothers and sisters' – and that means all Christians no matter to what Church they belong, for we are brothers and sisters in Christ. The prayer continues by asking God's mercy on 'all who have left this world in your friendship'. Again we see the catholicity of the Church; she cares for all who have died no matter what their belief may have been. If, in some way, they were in God's friendship, we have hope.

This great prayer of thanksgiving ends by stating the solemn truth that everything comes from the Father, through the working of the Son, by the power of the Spirit. The great 'Amen' should thunder back from the people, showing that they utterly and completely agree with all that has just been presented to them.

7

Give Us This Day

 Having called to mind and made present the great events that gave us new life in Christ, we now prepare to eat the eucharistic meal. We wish to identify ourselves with what we have celebrated. We have called the sacrifice of Christ to mind, now we call the Last Supper to mind, and by eating and drinking the sacred species, we unite ourselves to the saving act of the Lord.

Every year the Jews would call to mind the great saving event of the Old Testament. They did this by celebrating a meal, exactly similar to the one they ate on the night before they left Egypt. On that great night each household was instructed to take an umblemished lamb from the flock, slaughter it and mark the doorpost and lintels of the house where the meal was to be taken with some of the lamb's blood. Any house with this sign on its doorpost, would be passed over by the angel sent to bring death to the first born of each household.

Hence the feast celebrated every year after this was known as the Passover Feast.

The symbolism of the Feast is very marked, and the same symbolism is applied to Jesus. He was referred to by John the Baptist as 'the Lamb of God'. He was the Lamb without blemish who humbly allowed himself to be sacrificed for us all. A Christian is someone marked with the blood of the Lamb; we are singled out as people bought at a great price and therefore owned by God. The evil angels cannot actually touch us, unless we give them permission to do so. How fitting it is that Jesus introduced the eucharistic meal at the time when he and his apostles were celebrating the Passover. The great event by which the Jews celebrated their deliverance was used by Jesus to be the memorial meal by which we would call to mind our deliverance from the power of Satan. Jesus commanded us: 'Do this in memory of me.'

The Lord's Prayer

To help us prepare for the eucharistic meal, the Church puts on our lips the prayer that the Lord taught us. The very first word shows us that we are not here praying as individuals but as a People. It is God's plan for salvation that we be a people, a nation set apart, a body, united and vivified by the life of the Son. We are not united in the same way as members of a club are, we actually form one living body. That is why sins against each other are so harmful.

The reference to 'our daily bread' means both the bread we need every day and the bread of heaven

70

given to us ordinary mortals for our spiritual lives, bread which we share in common. Saying Grace before meals is a help to remind us in our busy day how we depend on God and each other for our daily food. If there was no sun, no rain, no soil – how could we grow our food? If we had no farmers to till the land, sow the seed and harvest the crops – who would grow the food for us? If there were no markets, no traders, no sailors, no drivers – how would the food get to us? How easily we take so much for granted, which causes so much labour and work! Rightly we ask pardon for our offences, and we even dare to stipulate that we receive pardon in the same measure that we grant it to those who offend us. We end by begging God to protect us from all evil.

The priest continues after this beautiful prayer by asking that we be delivered from every evil. What a beautiful prayer of trust in the goodness of God that is. Evil can come to us in all sorts of forms and we simply ask God to deliver us from them all. This is a clear statement that we believe that God is the master of the whole universe. A clear belief that he is the One in charge.

The priest continues, 'Keep us free from sin' – again the prayer teaches us that it is God who saves us from sin. We certainly have to avoid putting ourselves in vulnerable positions, but it is God who saves us through the mighty work of Jesus Christ.

'Protect us from all anxiety.' What an evil, anxiety can be! We fret and worry and live as though God was absent, remote or powerless. Anxiety can eat away at the very heart of the gospel which tells us 'to fear not'. Anxiety can reduce us to a state of unbelief – and that is a serious place to be. The peace that Christ offers us is not the peace of this world, where all goes well, all is in harmony and we feel buoyed up with pleasure and satisfaction. The peace of Christ means to have utter trust in his Lordship. It is not a confidence that he is going to remove all our problems, though of course he is perfectly able to do so and may do so, it is a trust that he can make these problems life-giving. It is a peace that can exist in the midst of trial, a peace that rests on the promise: 'Be brave, I have overcome the world' (Jn 16:33).

The Peace

As we approach the eucharistic meal together the Church seems to wish to bring home the lesson that too often we are divided, so she makes us show the sign of unity and forgiveness. Vatican II wisely restored the kiss of peace to the whole congregation. At one time it was restricted to the clergy and servers, but now the whole people at Mass are encouraged to show this sign. It has been suggested that it is artificial to make this gesture to people we do not know, but then we do not hesitate to kneel next to people at communion whom we do not know, and receive the same Lord into our hearts. Because we are Christians, we all share in the same life, and the same food is at that moment nourishing us all. I know a very sad story involving an alcoholic, who, having stopped his drinking through the great work of AA, decided to return to Church. He had been away for many years and he felt a certain apprehension as he returned. Vatican II was still being introduced and when the time for the kiss of peace came, this person turned expectantly to the person next to him to extend the peace and was told 'I do not do that'. Sadly the remark was taken personally and the alcoholic was not seen in that church again.

The Breaking of Bread

For bread to be eaten, it needs to be broken; for wine to be drunk, it needs to be poured out. Ideally the bread used at Mass should be large and bread-like, needing to be broken so that it can be shared.

The bread we break has become the body of Christ, and as the priest breaks it we recall that Christ's body was broken so that we might be given life. After the priest has broken the bread, he places a small piece of it in the chalice saying, 'May this mingling of the body and blood of our Lord Jesus Christ bring eternal life to us who receive it'. This rite dates back to the fourth century, and we are reminded that as the sacramental separation of the body and blood portrayed the Lord's death, so the bringing together portrays the Lord's resurrection. Also this rite recalls an ancient custom whereby bishops expressed their unity in Christ with their priests and people by sending a small particle of the bread consecrated at their own Mass to be put into the chalice of the various communities.

We can recall in Scripture that it was often through the breaking of bread that the disciples recognized the Lord. There was, for example, the occasion when Jesus, unrecognized, joined the two disciples on the way to Emmaus, and although their hearts were burning within them they did not know

it was Jesus until he broke the bread at supper.
Another time was after Peter had spent a fruitless
night fishing; the Lord appeared on the shore and
told Peter to throw his nets to starboard. When all
the disciples had hauled the catch ashore, 'they
knew quite well it was the Lord. Then Jesus stepped
forward, took the bread and gave it to them, and
the same with the fish' (Jn 21:12,13). Here, the
breaking of bread was part of the process by which
the disciples recognized Jesus.

Another meaning to the words, 'Do this in
memory of me', is that we, too, need to be broken
and poured out for God and for others. How we
fight against such a thought. We would rather work
for the Lord, do great things for him, convert conti-
nents; but then whose glory are we seeking? The
glory of God revealed in the face of Christ is the
face of One broken, poured out, even wasted so
that others might live. 'Come follow me.' Are we
ready truly to follow Christ? So much spirituality
can be seeking our own glory. This is the originating
sin, the sin that refused to live the plan of God –
'be one as We are One' – and chose to live for the
ego – to live independently.

The Meal Aspect

A meal is a very intimate gift, and, sadly, many of
us have forgotten the deep meaning behind it.
When we are given a pair of shoes, we receive
something to use. It is the same with a book, we
now have something to use. If we receive money,
again we have something that we can use. But when
we receive food, we are given the wherewithal to

74

live. The giver is, in fact, saying to us: 'I want you to live.' This intimate sign is deepened when we go to the trouble of preparing and cooking the food. When we sit down and share the meal, we are saying: 'I want to draw life from the same source as you.' Jesus goes further than we can go, he becomes the food and the drink. He is saying to us: 'Not only do I want you to live, but I want you to live through Me.'

Communion

Jesus instructed us to eat his body and drink his blood, and so we boldly approach the altar, aware of our unworthiness, but encouraged by his invitation. Through the act of eating his body and drinking his blood, we unite ourselves with all we have just witnessed. We have offered ourselves to God under the signs of bread and wine, these gifts were accepted and transformed into the body and blood of the Lord as he gave himself for us through death when his body and blood were separated. We now unite ourselves with this body and with this blood, thus bringing them together again within us, signifying his triumph over death – his resurrection. It is in the power of this new resurrected life that we live in a new way.

The priest at the time of preparation for communion says a silent prayer which beautifully sums up all these truths. I feel it is a pity that it is said silently – it may be that that was only a recommendation for when the Mass was being sung, for the Agnus Dei would be sung at that time.

The prayer says:

Lord Jesus Christ, Son of the living God,
by the will of the Father
and the work of the Holy Spirit,
your death brought life to the world.
By your holy body and blood
free me from all my sins and from every evil.
Keep me faithful to your teaching,
and never let me be parted from you.

How important it is that we are faithful to the Lord's teaching and not other people's interpretation of it.

All who communicate express their belief and desire to belong to Christ and the expression of him, visible on earth, the Church. Jesus was insistent that we come to the table of the Lord united with each other:

If you are bringing your offering to the altar and there remember that your brother has something against you, leave your offering there before the altar, go and be reconciled with your brother first, and then come back and present your offering.

Matt 5:23–24

There are sins that arise out of the softness of our human• nature, sins of weakness – sudden anger, sudden sexual desires, sudden impatience. Immediately following, we are sorry, repentant. But there are also sins that arise out of the hardness of our nature, these are sins of deliberate hate, unforgiveness, harbouring grudges, persistent unlove – these are serious and, alas, can be hidden under a very respectable and pious exterior. We should think carefully before approaching the table of the Lord, if we are in such a state and if there is not even a flicker of regret. 'Come to me, all you who labour and are overburdened, and I will give you rest' (Matt 11:28). In order to receive this rest, our coming to the Lord must be with regret and sorrow over our state.

The Church encourages a pause after the time of communion so that we may ponder and be amazed at what has happened. This is a time for personal adoration and worship, a time of quite union, a time for each to be with the Master. A time of incredible intimacy.

8

The Dismissal

The final part of the Mass is brief and that is significant. We came together to be present to Christ's everlasting sacrifice. We have been touched and enriched by it, now we are sent back into the market-place to carry out in our daily lives what we have just celebrated.

The time after communion is a quiet time, a time when we reflect on the intimate union we now have with the Lord. A staggering gift has been given to us, and those of us who receive this sacrament frequently can easily fail to grasp the enormity of the moment. I remember the first time I brought communion to a sick person, I was terribly conscious of what I carried, and then it dawned on me, how much more intimate it was to receive the Lord into my heart than carry him in my hands. How badly many of us need to rise from our complacency and consciously grasp hold of these realities.

The communion antiphon, which may be sung, read aloud or read privately, very often is like a word direct from the Lord. It is amazing how frequently the Scripture verse quoted is particularly suited for us that day. Sadly, however, we often fail to realize how privileged we are to receive such words from God; perhaps it would help us to imagine how honoured we would be if a distinguished person visited our town and sent a personal message to us! I remember once hearing the story of a lady who asked a famous preacher if he had a word from the Lord for her, and his response was to hand her the Bible. I certainly know from my own experience how easy it is to fail to see that every word spoken by God is a personal word for us.

During the Mass, we have listened and fed on the Word of God read to us in the Scriptures, we have also fed on the Word of God made flesh and made bread for us.

The priest ends the Mass with a prayer of thanksgiving and then he dismisses the people with the words: 'Go, the Mass is ended.' The word Mass actually comes from the Latin words of dismissal: 'Ite, missa est' – meaning, 'Go, it is the dismissal' (the sending out). I am afraid it is not exactly known how this word of dismissal came to refer to the whole celebration.

Before the dismissal, the priest blesses the people and although he says, 'The Mass is ended', in a sense he is saying the Mass is continuing. Christ came with the intention of healing us and setting us free, but he also commissioned us to go out and bring that healing and freedom to others. So, empowered with renewed vigour and life which we have drawn from this banquet, we go out now literally to do, in memory of him, what he did for us – to be broken and poured out for others.

How Can
I Pray?

Introduction

◆━━━◆

THE WRITINGS OF THE BIBLE – the Scriptures –
are the Word of God. They are of supreme importance
to all Christians and to all who wish to know and
understand the meaning of Christianity. The Bible
should be in every Christian home. Every aspect of
Christian life and worship should reflect in some way
what God says to his people. Catholics have not always
been very good at reading and studying the Bible. In
1965 during the Second Vatican Council a document
on Scripture as the Word of God (*Dei Verbum*) was
published. This has had a marked effect in laying the
foundations for an official programme of encourage-
ment to Catholics to make the Bible central to their
lives.

Much has happened since then. Every public act of
worship has its readings from Scripture. Scripture (both
Old and New Testaments) has a significant place in
all religious education programmes, whether for adults
or for children. The lectionary for the readings at daily
and Sunday Mass covers a large amount of Scripture
during its three-year cycle. Familiar acts of devotion
like the Rosary and the Stations of the Cross have
become far more scripturally based.

The positive value of this is obvious enough. But it
has also meant that many Catholics have been thrown
in at the deep end. They are a little like the Ethopian

in his carriage on the way home from Jerusalem who was reading some Scripture. Philip the Deacon heard him and asked him if he understood what he was reading. 'How can I', the man said, 'unless I have someone to guide me?' (Acts 8:26–40). Most of us do need help if we are to understand what we are reading. It is not that the language of Scripture is particularly difficult; it is rather that its context is so often unfamiliar.

I warmly welcome this series of *Scripture for Living*. Its particular value is that it helps us to see how Scripture is relevant to our daily lives. There are many other books for scholars. This series is for ordinary Christians who treasure Scripture, know for certain that it is of fundamental importance, but who are not sure how to make sense of what they read or how to relate it to their daily lives and experiences.

The pattern of the series is story, bible passage, commentary, reflection and prayer. There is a natural progression in this. The writings in the Bible (which form a whole library really) are about people trying to recognise God in their lives. So the context is just everyday life – the stuff of story. Story leads on naturally to Scripture because Scripture is itself about life in all its variety. So it speaks of love and hate, success and failure, death and resurrection; almost every imaginable human failing and strength finds place in it, simply because it is about real people. The commentary is an aid to understanding. Then, since the ultimate purpose of Scripture is to lead people closer to God, the text finishes with a prayer which ties together what has gone before and shows how our daily lives can be enriched.

The series is ideal for use in groups as well as by individuals. I wish it every success.

+ DAVID KONSTANT
Bishop of Leeds

Preface

I FEEL SOMEWHAT SHY in being asked to write this book because I do not see myself as a successful prayer. I have struggled for years at prayer and have known much heartache and discouragement, and I have ended up with some very simple thoughts on the subject. I know when I pray that God is present. It makes no difference if I feel he is there. The fact is that he *is* there and he has promised to be there. The other important truth I have discovered is that prayer is not to be judged by what I have got out of it, nor even by what I have put into it; it does not matter if I have had great thoughts or no thoughts, for prayer is not really about thinking; what matters is whether I have tried to love the Lord.

Prayer for me is constantly relating to God. I try not to confine it to special moments, though obviously there are special times when I try deliberately to pray. I seek to make the whole of my life a relating to God. You cannot form a proper relationship with someone to whom you never speak. Prayer is a dialogue, with God speaking first. But how do we hear God speak? Some people actually do hear God's voice in some inexplicable way – I don't. The way he communicates with me is through nature, through Scripture, through the ups and downs of life. What manner of being must he be who made sunlight, colours, hills and rainbows? Whenever I look at something beautiful, I try to imagine that God is saying to me, 'Do you like this or that? I made it for you. Did you see the particular blue in the sky this morning or had you forgotten that it is my world you are living in?' Childish? I do not think so, but I agree it may not be the way everyone would or should want to think.

Of course God has a lot more to say than that he is the inventor of beauty. He speaks to us in our tragedies, in our disasters and moments of fear. He speaks to us in our failures, our guilt, our weaknesses. He speaks when we feel most small and lost.

What is most important is our basic picture or idea of God. If God for us is not a loving person, then we can project our own feelings on to him and imagine, for example, that our sense of guilt or smallness are God condemning us. In such instances we need to remember the words in Scripture, 'Neither shall I condemn you'.

We need to ponder all that God has said to us in the Bible, remembering that Scripture has many faces and that we must balance one passage with another; there are plenty of passages, for example, where God appears angry and even harsh, but there are many others where he appears the opposite. God cannot fit into human language, so we must not become preoccupied with words, for words change from one generation to the next, and in translations exact renderings cannot always be made. We need to remember rather that God's words are 'spirit and life' – they have the power to speak to the deepest yearnings of our hearts.

God has spoken to us and we are called to reflect seriously upon his words. We need to develop the art of listening, of discerning when it is our own voice speaking and when it is the Lord's. So do not bring too many of your own ideas to the word of God, but allow the word to speak to you. Ask guidance of the Holy Spirit and then persevere.

IAN PETIT OSB

The Singer and the Song

◆——————◆

A SONG EXISTS only as long as the singer chooses to sing it into being. Let's imagine for a moment that a song could have consciousness; in other words, could be aware of itself.

I expect its first reaction would be one of sheer delight and amazement at its own form of existence. What an extraordinary thing to have one's being stretched out over time. No one moment can contain all of you, so existence means being passed from second to second, with no stopping to enjoy the richer bits nor rushing over what seems more unpleasant. A song cannot be had all at once, it has to come moment by moment. It is the sum of all the moments, and yet each moment is not the whole song.

Songs rise and fall. Sometimes they ascend with a sense of majesty and awe, lifting us up to celestial heights, rising slowly from note to note. Others soar up rapidly like swallows in a summer sky and then come plummetting down leaving us all but breathless.

A song, gifted with consciousness, would be fascinated with itself. How it would delight in winging down the scales, rising to dizzy heights and crashing into growling depths. What moods! What wonder! What beauty!

Hopefully, one day, the song would begin to ask where it comes from. Clearly it does not cause itself to exist. It receives existence moment by moment, but where does the gift of being come from? No sooner has it received one moment than there is another offered, and so it goes on.

The time when the song begins to ask this fundamental question, would, I think, be a time of both vulnerability and joy. Vulnerability, because it would suddenly know its own fragility; it does not depend on itself for life. What if the one who makes it exist should cease to bring it into being? I am sure there would be a momentary wobble as the song discovers the truth of its dependence on another.

Yet a deeper, more joyful and more comforting thought would no doubt dawn – 'I do exist, therefore someone must want me to be'. What an extraordinary comfort for the song to know that it is wanted. Existence is not of its own making, another has chosen it and goes on choosing it. I am sure the song would then want to know something about the singer. Is he or she good, strong, wise, powerful, loving? Now the song would begin to look beyond itself towards the singer. What manner of being must he or she be?

But could a song learn anything about the singer? A song only has song-experience and could not begin even to wonder what the singer would be like.

The only way that this could happen would be for the singer to tell the song about himself or herself.

◄══════►

In the beginning God created heaven and earth. Now the earth was a formless void, there was darkness over the deep, with a divine wind sweeping over the waters . . .

God said, 'Let us make man in our own image, in the likeness of ourselves, and let them be masters of the fish of the sea, the birds of heaven, the cattle, all

*the wild animals and all the creatures that creep along
the ground.'*

> *God created man in the image of himself,*
> *in the image of God he created him,*
> *male and female he created them.*

*God blessed them, saying to them, 'Be fruitful, mul-
tiply, fill the earth and subdue it. Be masters of the
fish of the sea, the birds of heaven and all the living
creatures that move on earth.' God also said, 'Look,
to you I give all the seed-bearing plants everywhere
on the surface of the earth, and all the trees with seed-
bearing fruit; this will be your food. And to all the
wild animals, all the birds of heaven and all the living
creatures that creep along the ground, I give all the
foliage of the plants as their food.' And so it was. God
saw all he had made, and indeed it was very good.
Evening came and morning came: the sixth day.*

(Genesis 1: 1–2, 26–31)

God has made everything. He spoke and things suddenly came into being. The fact that they have
remained in being must mean that he continues to
speak, or sing, them. We could therefore say that he
is continually singing creation into being. I find this a
wonderful way to think of creation – as God's song.

We, of course, are among the things that God sings
into being. Each one of us is different, unique. God
has specially chosen us, and it is important for us to
remember that God never makes a mistake. We are
his invention, and he goes on inventing us at every
moment.

It is sad that so many of us often have very bad
pictures of ourselves. Certainly, we have made mistakes, done wrong things, but to judge ourselves by
our errors and misdeeds is to value ourselves by what

we do and not by what we are. We are the special
creation of God and as such we are of immense value.

I find it helpful sometimes to seek out a quiet place
to sit and just ponder from where my life is coming.
We certainly do not cause our own existence – if we
did that, then we could guarantee that we would see
the next century in. We need to try and be aware of
receiving existence as a gift and let ourselves be
amazed that God has chosen to create us. We know
how much we like to be thanked when we give something to someone, so it perhaps isn't too difficult to
imagine the joy God must feel when we thank him for
calling us into being.

Returning to the idea of the song, imagine how foolish it would be if the song turned round to the singer
and said, 'I do not need you'. What an insult that would
be! That is what sin is. Sin is us saying to the God
who creates us, 'I do not need you'. *All* sin involves
us trying to be independent of God.

I realise that when we pray it is not easy for us to
focus on these deeper truths. We live in a busy world
and there are so many demands made upon us. There
is always this need and that, there is the constant
pressure of time. We are continually being pushed to
hurry and fit everything in. That is why it is so necessary to try and be still and stand back from life so that
we may look and see things in perspective.

Being still is difficult. Our minds are so active. We
may be used to 'thinking' about God, but prayer is
really more about 'loving' God and being open to him.
That is why it is good to try and become aware of the
actual moment we are living. To be conscious of what
we feel, be aware of what we sense at this very
moment. If we concentrate on experiencing all these
sensations as God speaking to us, we will find that our
attention can become focused. Hopefully, just as the
song did, we will begin to ask, 'Who is calling us into

being?' 'What is he like?' We will discover that we want to know our creator, and to build a relationship with him.

FOR REFLECTION

1. Do you want to discover and know God, the one who sings you into being?
2. Do you want to build a relationship with him?
3. Do you have a set time for prayer, or are you hoping to fit it in 'sometime', or do you leave it until you have some urgent need?
4. How much of your prayer time is spent in thanksgiving?
5. You may, like me, find it helpful to be quiet for a few minutes and concentrate on being open to God in the present moment – open, for example, to your own body, to what you see and hear around you.

PRAYER

Lord, you are the inventor of rainbows, fountains, butterflies and stars. You also chose to invent me. I thank you for my being. I am sorry that I have so misunderstood you – I have been so very blind.

I know you are listening to me right now and through your Son's cross you have forgiven me and your Holy Spirit brings me that forgiveness because I am asking for it. Help me to see you in every event of this day. You are my creator, and I say 'yes' to being your creature.

I make this prayer in the name of Jesus Christ your Son. Amen.

Prayer as Listening

◆━━━━▶

MARTIN FELT very low as he tried with no success to keep his mind on God.

He had come on this prayer weekend at the suggestion of Gerard, his friend, who unfortunately had had to cry off at the very last minute. Martin wanted to cancel as well but Gerard had said that he really had no good excuse. So, very reluctantly, Martin had arrived. He knew, as soon as he got there, that he had made a mistake. He did not know a soul, he was by far the youngest, and he was the only man present. Also from what people were saying during the first meal, he felt he was among experts in the art of prayer. People were talking about St Teresa of Avila, St John of the Cross and everyone was asking about a book just out written by a French mystic.

Martin seriously wanted to know more about prayer. Gerard had been on a similar weekend last year and had come home full of it. This had aroused Martin's interest. Martin was 23 and he had felt that there must be much more to prayer than long lists of requests. He had learnt to say the rosary at school, but he never got very much from it. There was always the problem of trying to think of one of the mysteries while you were saying something else. So, because of Gerard's enthusiasm, Martin decided he had better take some steps to learn more about prayer.

The priest, Father Peter, was bald and rather fat, a jolly sort who seemed to have lots to say and many stories to tell. During the first talk on the Friday evening he said, and it seemed as though he said it almost by chance, that prayer involved listening to God not just talking to him. Though Martin would not have said that that was a totally new idea to him, in some way it struck him. In fact it struck him so forcibly that he decided, there and then, that he would spend some time next day listening to God.

So here he was in the chapel and he was feeling very low because he did not, or could not, hear God. He had been there for twenty minutes; he had promised to spend half an hour, and nothing had happened. He had started off by asking God to speak to him and had asked pardon for never really trying to hear him before. If the truth were known, he never had expected God to speak to him. Surely God only spoke to exceptionally holy people. Anyway, the priest had said that a large part of prayer was listening to God, so he was giving it a try.

He had been in the chapel about ten minutes when he had heard the door open at the back. For a fleeting moment he wondered if that was God coming in to talk with him, then he dismissed the idea remembering that God was already in the chapel and besides God did not come in through doors.

How incredibly difficult it was to listen and not get distracted. How do you listen to nothing? Was God going to speak in a solemn voice? It was all very well to say that we need to listen, but just how do you do that? He had heard a bus going down the street outside, and half wished that he was on it, back in his normal world. Every now and then the radiators gave a creak, or he could hear someone calling in the distance. A dog barked. An aeroplane flew overhead. In fact he heard nearly everything but God.

Because he could not hear God, he found his thoughts wandering here, there and everywhere. He tried picturing God, but soon gave that up because God is spirit, he has no body, no shape. It was rather difficult picturing someone with no shape. He then tried picturing Jesus. This wasn't successful either because the statue of the Sacred Heart, not far from where he was kneeling, was very different to the Jesus on the cross high above the altar. It was all extremely confusing.

Finally he sat down and hoped that it was still prayer even if he had ceased to kneel. Kneeling was all very well but when you have not done a lot of it, it can be painful.

For these last few minutes, which seemed to go even slower than all the others, he decided to try and think of nothing, hoping that if he succeeded God might pop into his mind. Needless to say this was a total failure. Martin, by now, was feeling frustrated, even a little angry and annoyed. After all he had come on this retreat against his will, he had tried to listen to God. Had God not noticed? Was he really there? If so, why did he say nothing? While he was thinking these thoughts he found that he was looking at the lectern standing in the sanctuary. On it stood the book with all the readings for the Masses throughout the year. It suddenly dawned on Martin that God had spoken and he was asking him: 'Why have you never listened to what I have already said?'

God had communicated with Martin and had been doing it for some time, but Martin had not recognised him because he had never really been listening in the right way.

⟷

Now, the boy Samuel was serving Yahweh in the presence of Eli; in those days it was rare for Yahweh to speak; visions were uncommon. One day, it happened that Eli was lying down in his room. His eyes were beginning to grow dim, he could no longer see. The lamp of God had not yet gone out, and Samuel was lying in Yahweh's sanctuary, where the ark of God was, when Yahweh called, 'Samuel! Samuel!' He answered, 'Here I am,' and, running to Eli, he said, 'Here I am, as you called me.' Eli said, 'I did not call. Go back and lie down.' So he went and lay down. And again Yahweh called, 'Samuel! Samuel!' He got up and went to Eli and said, 'Here I am, as you called me.' He replied, 'I did not call, my son; go back and lie down.' As yet, Samuel had no knowledge of Yahweh and the word of Yahweh had not yet been revealed to him. Again Yahweh called, the third time. He got up and went to Eli and said, 'Here I am, as you called me.' Eli then understood that Yahweh was calling the child, and he said to Samuel, 'Go and lie down, and if someone calls say, "Speak, Yahweh; for your servant is listening." '

(1 Samuel 3:1–9)

⬤⟶

Clearly, Samuel did not recognise God when he spoke to him. Three times he thought it was the High Priest Eli speaking to him. So it is with us, we often do not recognise God when he speaks to us.

Martin had the same problem. The priest had reminded him that prayer involved listening as well as speaking. But Martin needed to be taught how to listen. He expected God to speak in audible words; whereas all the time Martin needed to be reminded that God had already spoken many words and he, Martin, had not paid very much attention to them.

How can you have a relationship with someone you do not know? I live near a railway station and frequently I see one of the porters of the station walking in the street where I live. I do not know his name, I know he is a porter but I do not know what he thinks, what he likes, what makes him happy. To find this out I would need to talk to him and let him talk to me. Before I can have a relationship with him, I would need to know him.

It is the same with God. Too often we try to talk to the God we do not know. We may imagine we know some things about this God, but often what we know bears little resemblance to the real God. We get ideas about God, ideas which are often of our own making. We need to remember that no thought that any of us have *is* God. God cannot be caught or captured by a thought; no thought of ours has got him wrapped up.

We need to allow God to tell us about himself, and even though our minds will not be big enough to grasp the full picture, at least we will not be feeding on some fantasy but on the truth. We need to fill our minds with all that God has told us. We need to ponder and listen to what he has said. In Scripture we learn all that God has done for us human beings, and the Church brings out the appropriate readings for the liturgical seasons, helping us to hear what God is saying to us at the relevant times.

But Scripture is not the only way that God speaks to us. We need to learn how to read the signs of the times. What is God saying through the state of the world at the present moment? We need to listen to the moods within ourselves. We need to be able to recognise fears, sudden moments of anxiety – what is God saying to us through these things?

Martin was not able to see why he was fearful of going on that weekend retreat. He was unaware of the spiritual battle raging within him. Being ignorant of God's word, of what God had already said, Martin was no threat to Satan. Martin was not an evil person, he was nice, pleasant and respectable; but he did not know the true God; rather, he knew certain things about God, and as such he was no problem to Satan. But if he should learn the truth, then he might tell others. So Satan played upon Martin, and he sensed a great fear and reluctance about the retreat.

Once a person becomes open to the fact that God has actually said quite a lot, and that he still speaks, then that person needs to learn to discern between his or her own promptings and those of God. Imaginative people can easily be led astray. We have to face the fact that we can still be ambitious, even in the realm of the spirit and spiritual pride is very deadly. In John 10:4, Jesus said that his sheep would follow him 'because they know his voice.' In 1 John 4 we are warned to test the spirits. We may get beautiful and apparently holy ideas, but we need to look and see if we are just building ourselves up, imagining we are God's gift to the world, or are we allowing Jesus to be built up? 'Any spirit which acknowledges Jesus Christ, come in human nature, is from God' (1 John 4:2).

Listening is not easy. Samuel was told to say: 'Speak, Yahweh; for your servant is listening.' We tend to say: 'Listen, Lord, your servant is speaking.' We live in a world full of noise and bustle, and when we settle down to pray, our minds continue to whirl around. Obviously we cannot just stop and empty our minds. The mind cannot not think. You might as well command the eye not to see. But it is good to try and still the mind by giving it something to do. Try and fix your mind on the now, the present moment. Be conscious of what you hear, what you feel now. This helps to quieten us down and we become aware of how unaware we really are. The present moment is the only moment that touches us. We can live our lives fretting about the future, worrying about the past and never being truly alive in the present. Being conscious of our breathing, our bodies, can lead us on to consciousness of the gift of life. Who gives us life? In this sort of stillness, we can begin to hear God calling our name.

FOR REFLECTION

1. When you pray, how do you do it? Do you do all the speaking or do you listen?
2. List the different ways in which you hear God.
3. Do you have a set way of praying or do you just hope you will get 'lift-off'?
4. Has your way of praying changed over the years? Can you see why it has changed?

PRAYER

Lord speak your word over my deafness and blindness. Teach me how to listen and hear you in everything that you have made. Lord, stop the chatter of my mind, where I live my desires. Teach me to long for your kingdom, where your will is what is important. Give me ears to hear your still quiet voice. Amen.

Praying through Creation

I MUST HAVE BEEN about 12 years old when a school friend of mine, whose father was posted in Gibraltar, told me about his summer holidays on the Rock. He must have had a way with words for I know I was enraptured as he described the boat journey, the arrival in blazing sunshine, the narrow streets, the monkeys on the Rock, the oranges and grapes, the swimming and the hot summer days. Here was something completely different to my English experience and I fell in love with travel, the tropics and sunshine all in one fell swoop.

The chances of my travelling abroad were very remote, for foreign travel had not become accessible to ordinary people, so I made do with what I had. I became interested in seasons, and I would watch for the shadow of the sun to decrease, showing me that summer was approaching. I became aware of what grew around me, and wondered what it would be like to live in a place where oranges and grapes grew out-of-doors. I do not know if my memory deceives me or if the summers of long ago were really that fine, but I recall hot summer days with swallows wheeling in blue skies, jugs of cold lemonade, Wall's ice creams bought from a man on a bicycle, long summer evenings. Quite unknown to my friend a whole new world had opened up for me. I met something, or was it someone, in this new world. I could stand for hours looking at hills, cornfields neatly stacked with stooks, waterfalls, flowers. I had become a country man, a man of nature, though I lived in the suburbs of London.

I wonder, now, if I was meeting God then but simply never recognised him. The God I met in church seemed to me rather dull, he seemed full of rules and regulations, and was rather against everything that appealed to me. So I had a fear of him. What I met in the fields and hills filled me with awe, reverence, excitement and wonder. I felt an urge to kick off my shoes and go and dance in the long grass, but I was a town boy, so I never dared do such a strange thing. Now I can say that that would have been a form of worship.

It has taken most of my life to bring these two ways of meeting God together. Alas, my early church experience had so coloured my ideas of God that when I did meet him in the fields I did not recognise him. What a joy it was when, later in life, I read in the psalms such marvelous praise of God for the wonders he has created. How poetic the book of Job is as he describes the mysteries of creation. How important it is that we listen to the God who communicates with us through such things as colour, shape and size.

◆━━━▶

Bless Yahweh, my soul,
Yahweh, my God, how great you are!
Clothed in majesty and splendour,
wearing the light as a robe!

You stretch out the heavens like a tent,
build your palace on the waters above,
making the clouds your chariot,
gliding on the wings of the wind,

appointing the winds your messengers,
flames of fire your servants.

You fixed the earth on its foundations,
for ever and ever it shall not be shaken;
you covered it with the deep like a garment,
the waters overtopping the mountains.

At your reproof the waters fled,
at the voice of your thunder they sped away,
flowing over mountains, down valleys,
to the place you had fixed for them;
you made a limit they were not to cross,
they were not to return and cover the earth.

(Psalm 104:1–9)

I have often seen some work of art and have felt a desire to meet the person who could create such beauty. In some way that beauty resided in the artist and I wanted to know him or her. I have sometimes had my wish and been able to meet the person in question, and I have to confess that occasionally I have been disappointed. But somewhere, deep down inside them, that beauty must have resided.

So, what of God who surrounds us with his works of art? What manner of being must he be who can create stars and scatter them in such vast spaces? The psalms describe him as marshalling them and calling each one by its name. Standing at night and staring into the clear sky, fills one with awe and wonder.

What manner of being must he be who created colour and put it everywhere? How dull life would be if everything appeared as a black and white photo. I find it helpful to look at things and try and imagine them as shades of black and white, and then suddenly I become aware of their colour. I am continually

surprised and delighted by the world God has created,
surprised by the shapes, colour, beauty, growth, richness and variety. I find it amazing to think that no
two sunsets are ever the same, to think of the seeds
that are scattered – how prodigious is God's bounty.

For me, God is forever nudging us with his creation.
I know every time I go in an aeroplane, it is as good
as a retreat. I admit there is the thought that this might
be my last act – that is sobering and not to be rejected;
but once I am airborne I become like a child with a
new toy. What a wonder it is to suddenly have your
horizons extended. How fascinating it is to look at
things from above. How tiny we humans are. Also
what excitement there is to view the clouds from
above – they have such marvellous shapes and are so
white!

My meeting with God as the creator of the universe
has done much for me. Early impressions of God are
significant for if they are not palatable, then everything
from then on has a bias. Because the God I heard about
in church seemed so unattractive, then everything that
was connected with him became unappealing to me.
My meeting with God in nature had the advantage
that I did not recognise that this was God whom I was
meeting. Having fallen in love with him unconsciously, it was quite startling to learn later on that I
had fallen in love with God!

Although I didn't realise it at the time, I had actually
been praying as a child when I met God in nature. I
had been unconsciously thanking him and worshipping him for all his wonders. Now, as an adult, I know
that it is God I see in the beauty around me and I am
able to respond more fully.

Prayer becomes a response to the God who speaks
first to me, and one of the ways he speaks is through
the natural world.

FOR REFLECTION

1. How conscious are you of the beauty around you?
2. Do you just admire beauty in nature or does it lead you on to thinking about God?
3. Do you thank God for his world?

PRAYER

I bless you Father for all that you have invented. I thank you that you included me in your plan. Help me to be a good steward here on earth. Amen.

Praying through Other People

SHE GOT ON THE BUS about two stops after I did. All this must have happened at least 40 years ago, so many of the details have been lost, but the impact of the encounter is still as clear to me as if it happened yesterday.

She must have been well into her forties – may be as much as fifty – but to my young eyes she was old. She was dumpy, her hair was dyed blond and she was highly made-up. What stands out most clearly in my memory is her hat. I cannot remember so much the shape, it was black but it was simply covered with bright red cherries. They hung all over it and at the slightest movement they bounced up and down. I can remember thinking: 'My good lady, why go out dressed up like that?' – and I dismissed her as a foolish old woman.

The seats on the buses in those days ran the length of the bus, looking in, thus giving plenty of room for standing passengers during the rush hour. She sat down, not quite opposite me, a little to my right, and as the bus lurched off the cherries started to dance and bounce.

On my right sat another woman with a small child on her lap and it did not take him long to notice these shining cherries and he stretched out his chubby hands towards them, opening and closing his little fists. Soon the woman with the cherry hat noticed the little boy stretching out affectionately towards her, and so she nodded her head, and the cherries began a wild dance. Squeals of delight came from the child. The more he squealed, the more she nodded, and soon all the people around were drawn into this happy encounter.

This continued for several stops, then the woman beside me, doing her best to control her enraptured son, said to the woman with the hat: 'Have you any children of your own?' I can still see her smiling under that hat of hers as she said: 'Oh, yes, I had one but I lost him.'

I do not know the story. I do not know how it happened, she never told us, she just sat there under her funny hat, smiling and nodding at the little boy who was all but convulsed with laughter and joy. All I know is that I suddenly saw into that good woman's life, I saw behind the funny exterior, I saw into the sanctuary of her being, and I felt very ashamed at my rash judgement.

I wanted to go and kneel in front of her and tell her of my misjudgement – but you just do not do that sort of thing.

I know I got off that bus a wiser young man than I had got on it. She never spoke one single word to me, yet she taught me a lesson that I have never forgotten. 'Do not judge. You do not know what lies behind the pair of eyes you look into. Everyone has their story.'

<hr>

Do not judge, and you will not be judged; because the judgements you give are the judgements you will get, and the standard you use will be the standard used for you. Why do you observe the splinter in your brother's eye and never notice the great log in your own? And how dare you say to your brother, 'Let me take that splinter out of your eye,' when, look, there

is a great log in your own? Hypocrite! Take the log
out of your own eye first, and then you will see clearly
enough to take the splinter out of your brother's eye.
(Matthew 7:1–5)

◆━━━━◆

We must not confine God to 'holy times' or 'holy
places'. Jesus lived his life both in the market place
and in the hills where he went to pray. God is always
present to us, communicating with us; it is we who
have consciously to make ourselves aware of his presence. Stupidly we can tend to imagine God is only
present when we think of him.

God manifests himself in many ways and one way
is through the people he has made. We need to learn
the art of penetrating beyond the external to find the
singer of each particular song.

We need to remember that other people are other
people – they are not extensions of ourselves, so we
cannot and must not manipulate them. They are other;
and it is not wrong to be other. They will see things
differently from us, and that is of value because we
cannot see all sides to things.

God has made each one of us and each is different,
unique. Life, with all its ups and downs, forms and
shapes us, can even wound us. So when we meet
people we meet someone chosen by God, who never
makes mistakes, but we are also meeting someone
who has a story to tell, and that story will have left
its imprints, both good and bad.

I was different from the woman with the funny hat.
Surely the hat was not funny to her; maybe the fault
was in me. My mistake was to fail to let her be different, and to judge her for being different.

Again, I come back to basic questions – 'Who is this
God to whom we pray? What is he like?' We can make
God into our own image and likeness. We can forget

he made the world and imagine he is only in churchy
places. We can domesticate him, shut him up in a box,
put him out of reach, not expect to see him in the
market place. Nowadays we see posters of beautiful
land or seascapes with some scriptural quotation on
them, and while that is fine, again, we must not confine God only to the beautiful. When Jesus came on
earth, he did not shun sharing our weakness. He
so identified himself with our sorrows that Isaiah
prophesied:

> As many people were aghast at him
> – he was so inhumanly disfigured
> that he no longer looked like a man –
> so many nations will be astonished
> and kings will stay tight-lipped before him
> seeing what had never been told them,
> learning what they had not heard before.
>
> (Isaiah 52:14,15)

Is the God we pray to only the One we meet in Scripture, or is he also the One we meet in others hidden in
a thousand different guises? Sometimes so 'disfigured'
that we do not recognise him.

When the Lord tells us not to judge, he does not
mean that we should never use our critical faculties.
We need to listen to the whole of what the Lord has
said to us. He certainly tells us not to judge, but he
also tells us to be 'cunning as snakes, and yet innocent
as doves' (Matthew 10:16). If someone does wrong, I
am not called to overlook the wrong, to pretend it is
not there. I have to be honest, I may even have to
correct the wrong. What the Lord asks of us is not
to judge the person, who does wrong, but to try and
understand. We are quite ready to find excuses when
we do wrong, but are we as ready to excuse others?

So God comes to us in other people and therefore
other people can help us in our prayer. They give us

glimpses into the God we cannot see. The woman on the bus had some tragic experience, she had lost her child, I do not know the details. Such an experience would have left a mark. Who is to know whether the red hat was some gallant attempt on her part to face life again and appear healed? How thoughtless it was of me to have judged her. She never spoke a word to me, but through her God taught me not to judge. 'You do not know the story that lies behind the face you look at.'

FOR REFLECTION

1. Do you learn about God through other people?
2. Can you think of people who have helped you understand God better? What was the particular way they helped?
3. Do you look at other people on buses or trains and wonder what their story is, or do you fail even to notice them?
4. When did you last ask someone you live with, what it is like being them?

PRAYER

Father, what must you be like who can create so many different things and people, and yet manifest yourself through each of them? I thank you for all whom you have put into my life. Many I did not choose, but you chose them. Give me your eyes to see them as you do. What a difference that would make to me.

I ask with confidence because I ask this in the name of your Son. Amen.

Hearing God through Life's Hurts

FROM THE KITCHEN Elizabeth heard the key turn in the front door. This was the moment that she had been dreading ever since Michael, her husband, had phoned her, shortly after 3 o'clock to tell her that he had been made redundant. It was not a bolt out of the blue, for three weeks ago it had been put out that there were going to be drastic cut backs in the firm. Michael had then sunk into a deep gloom and had been going backwards and forwards between fear and anxiety, and then anger and resentment. 'Why did God seem to have it in for them?', was the question he kept asking. Elizabeth did not know how to answer that, for it was true, they were having quite a run of difficulties. Their first born, a little boy, had been dead on birth. That had been just over two years ago. Michael had been shattered by that, and then when Debby arrived, she obviously was not a healthy child and gave them both much anxiety, but clearly Michael continued to grieve that he had lost his son.

They were both Catholics, though Elizabeth was the stronger of the two. She had tried to comfort Michael and had talked to him about accepting God's will and there was a need to 'carry one's cross'. Michael's answer had always been, 'But why pick on us?', and

Elizabeth did not know the answer to that. And that is why she dreaded having to face him now that the worst had happened.

He looked so vulnerable and crushed, standing there in the hall. She went to him and held him close. It was a relief that he allowed her to do this and nothing was said.

Thoughts raced through Elizabeth's mind as she stood there with her arms around her husband. 'Why, Lord, did you not hear our prayers? What about those Masses I attended ever since we heard of the threat of redundancy?' What of all those prayers, said here and there as she had gone about her daily chores?

Father Smith, their parish priest, had preached a beautiful sermon only last Sunday on the love of God. It had been quite moving, but now it all seemed like hot air. Both Elizabeth and Michael had turned to this loving God in their trouble and he had not answered their cry for help. Elizabeth grew cold and her mind seemed to suddenly sweat with fear as she saw where her thoughts were leading her. 'My God! What would they do if she ceased to believe?' She had always felt, somehow, that it was right to believe in God and Christianity and all that. She had grown up with the idea that God was good and that he could be trusted and that if you asked his help he would 'hear your prayer'. All that now looked very shallow, untrue, yes even superstitious. Perhaps it was all a con.

Michael broke in on these thoughts saying, 'But why? Why? Why?', and they both wept there standing in the hall.

It was old Alice Micklethorpe who gave the first glimmer of hope a few days later. She heard of the bad news, had donned her hat, coat and gloves and come round to comfort the young couple.

'Don't be silly, deary, God never sends troubles. Troubles come from all sorts of places, but never from the good God. Deary me – what a thought!', and she shook her old head causing her double chin to wobble. 'This great God of ours, somehow permits bad things to happen', and she rolled her tired eyes as though it pained her to think such a thought, 'but he never causes them', and she was quite emphatic over that. 'What a terrible day it is for caterpillars when they start to become butterflies. They nearly cease to be. They are stripped of everything they had and have to lie tied up in a cocoon-like pod for weeks. But, look what happens in the end.' And again the chins swayed back and forth as though to add weight to her words.

'Was this God's answer to all those prayers', thought Elizabeth, because from then on Michael began to grow calm. It was not a sudden release, but at least there was a glimmer. Nothing was actually said, but when Alice got up to leave after giving her words of wisdom, Michael hugged her.

He called the people and his disciples to him and said, 'If anyone wants to be a follower of mine, let him renounce himself and take up his cross and follow me. Anyone who wants to save his life will lose it; but anyone who loses his life for my sake, and for the sake of the gospel, will save it. What gain, then, is it for anyone to win the whole world and forfeit his life? And indeed what can anyone offer in exchange for his life? For if anyone in this sinful and adulterous generation is ashamed of me and of my words, the Son of man will also be ashamed of him when he comes in the glory of his Father with the holy angels.'
(Mark 8:34–38)

When tragedies hit us, it is very hard to believe in the love of God. Times of prayer become very difficult because we are wondering just how God could let something like this happen to us. Deep down we feel a resentment, and yet at the same time we feel guilty about not wanting what has happened and feel a bit small in arguing against God. The trouble is that we know he is always right and somehow it does not seem fair.

All sorts of problems can arise from this. Either we decide to continue with God, but our attitude becomes one of suspicion and fear, and we will not want to go very deep with him, or we will decide to drop him completely and go our own way.

Elizabeth and Michael had obviously been taught the necessity of carrying their crosses, but exactly what that meant had not been made clear to them. They mistakenly thought every hardship that came their way had to be willingly embraced as God's will.

I think many of us, like Elizabeth and Michael, have received bad teaching about the will of God. We've all been told, 'This is your cross' or 'It is God's will', but is that always true? We must not call all suffering the 'cross', because the 'cross' is any suffering that comes *because* we have decided to follow the Lord. See in the biblical passage that Jesus says *if* anyone *wants* be a disciple then he (or she) will have to suffer certain things. This does not mean that other sufferings cannot be used meritoriously, but we should not call them the 'cross'.

I believe there is an important difference between God's will and God's permissive will (i.e. what God *allows* to happen). I don't believe God willed that Michael should be made redundant, lose his little son and have a daughter with ill health. It is true, God could have prevented these things, but he seems to allow them because he sees how these very evils can be used to produce growth and good. Because Michael thought of God as sending him all these trials, he felt a deep resentment and hostility towards God; he was reluctant to simply accept these things and offer them up. But once Alice's idea of God being on his side took root in him, there started a new growth, which might never have begun if he had not suffered in the first place.

We have no abiding city here. We were not made to be here forever, and we have got it wrong if we think we have a right to a trouble-free existence on earth. Sin has thrown everything out of balance, but God can use these imbalances to produce patience, love, understanding and gentleness.

Honest and genuine prayer must involve expressing our hurt and questions to God. He is big enough to cope with them, and we often grow most as Christians through our response to setbacks and suffering. We clearly should not look for hardship, but when it comes it *can* be used for good.

FOR REFLECTION

1. Do you see misfortune as God's will for you?
2. Do you ever express your deeper feelings to God or do you feel that would be wrong?
3. Can you see the difference between carrying your cross and bearing ordinary suffering?

PRAYER

Lord, I want to trust my life and all that I have into your care. Forgive me, for I have often doubted your love, I have feared that you would take from me everything that means most to me. But, Lord, that is how I learnt about you. Forgive us all for our blindness. Amen.

Hearing God through Weakness

'WHY DOES GOD make it so difficult to know him? Why can't he just appear to us, or do something staggering and make everyone believe? Why has he got to hide, to make things obscure? Why does he allow us, his creatures, almost to be able to prove that he does not exist? Why does he sit up in heaven and never move a muscle to prove people wrong?'

These thoughts and many other angry ones were buzzing through Jeremy's mind as he walked home after his evening visit with Paul to the local pub. They met there most evenings and they had become good friends. Jeremy was a believer, Paul was not.

That evening Paul had been dismantling all Jeremy's arguments for God's existence. It was not that Paul was out to destroy Jeremy's faith, he really was just sharing his views and honest doubts. The trouble was they were very convincing. He argued that with the advance of science and knowledge all the reasons why primitive people believed in a god had now been proved false. Thunder and lightening were not signs of a mighty god storming around the heavens, they could all be explained scientifically. 'You see, Jeremy, we just do not need to have a god to explain all these mysteries. All that once argued for the existence of a god has now been uncovered.' Jeremy could see the logic behind this reasoning, but deep down he knew it was not the last word. What annoyed him was he could not find the last word.

On his way home, Jeremy found angry thoughts rising up within him. If he had been ruthlessly honest with himself, he would have admitted that for a moment he had touched the first glimmerings of a thought that perhaps all that he held dear and important might suddenly be proved to be false. Such a thought was immediately expelled – but it had been there and Jeremy somehow knew it.

'Why can't you manifest yourself?' It was as though he shouted that to the skies. Only this morning at Mass, the reading had begun, 'Oh, that you would tear the heavens open and come down' (Isaiah 64:1). 'Why sit up there, and let your creatures disprove your existence? You are meant to be a strong God full of power and glory. Why don't you do something? Is it that you cannot? Or is it that you do not really exist?' There, he had actually said the words for the moment Jeremy's world tottered and swayed, 'O God, what if . . .?'

◆━━━━➤

There he [Elijah] went into a cave and spent the night there. Then the word of Yahweh came to him saying, 'What are you doing here, Elijah?' He replied, 'I am full of jealous zeal for Yahweh Sabaoth, because the Israelites have abandoned your covenant, have torn down your altars and put your prophets to the sword. I am the only one left, and now they want to kill me.' Then he was told, 'Go out and stand on the mountain before Yahweh.' For at that moment Yahweh was going by. A mighty hurricane split the mountains and shattered the rocks before Yahweh. But Yahweh was not in the hurricane. And after the hurricane, an earthquake. But Yahweh was not in the earthquake. And

*after the earthquake, fire. But Yahweh was not in the
fire. And after the fire, a light murmuring sound. And
when Elijah heard this, he covered his face with his
cloak and went out and stood at the entrance of the
cave. Then a voice came to him, which said, 'What
are you doing here, Elijah?' He replied, 'I am full of
jealous zeal for Yahweh, God Sabaoth, because the
Israelites have abandoned your covenant, have torn
down your altars and put your prophets to the sword.
I am the only one left and now they want to kill me.'
'Go,' Yahweh said, 'go back by the same way to the
desert of Damascus. You must go and anoint Hazael
as king of Aram.'*

(1 Kings 19:9–15)

Jeremy felt frustrated because as Paul talked, it seemed
to him that God, as it were, was allowing the human
race with its brilliance to prove it had no need of him.

Jeremy believed that God existed, but he seemed
quite unable to give arguments to support his convic-
tion. Paul, on the other hand, was showing how primitive people had needed something to explain what they
saw in the universe; science had now provided the
answers and God was not needed as an explanation.
Deep down Jeremy had to concede that God had done
himself out of a job, by letting the human mind
develop so well in its understanding of the universe.
It seemed now, that God had very little to commend
him. What could Jeremy say in the face of all this?
That was why he felt frustrated on his way home and
he began wishing that God would stop hiding himself
and come out and do something mind-blowing.

I am sure we have all wrestled with the question,
why does God apparently hide? The very power and
splendour of the universe convinced early civilisations,

that God existed, but now science claims to be able to explain the wonders of the world.

In the passage from the book of Kings, God is showing us that he does not always reveal himself in might and dazzling power but that he can come in hiddenness and gentleness. It was not in the hurricane or the earthquake or the fire that he came to Elijah, but in a soft breeze.

Jesus, who told us that to see him was to see the Father, conquered Satan, not in the clashing of swords or with stupendous demonstrations of power, but by allowing himself to be seemingly defeated. He appeared to have downed his weapons and offered no resistance – he was 'like a lamb led to the slaughter house' (Isaiah 53:7). It is the strange story of victory through apparent weakness, summer following winter, death being followed by rising.

God so loved the world that he sent his Son into it. He was not born into a royal or powerful family; he did not become a Roman. He chose to belong to a poor nation, quite small and occupied by a foreign power. He chose to be a nobody, an unprivileged person, someone who could be done away with without anyone raising a voice in protest. He came to share in our human weakness.

> Who, being in the form of God,
> did not count equality with God
> something to be grasped.
> But he emptied himself,
> taking the form of a slave,
> becoming as human beings are.
> (Philippians 2:6–7)

We tend to think of God in terms of glory, power, splendour, and while all that is true it is not the whole picture, there is another side to him. He came among us in weakness.

It is only through prayer that we can come to know both the power and the weakness of God. He wishes to encourage us when we feel confused, bewildered as to why he, who has all power, does not act in some powerful way to convince this unbelieving world. His ways are not our ways, and he can draw his purposes out of very unlikely situations. Things that seem to us useless, even disasters, he can use and make life giving. I am sure we all know stories in which what seemed totally hopeless, in the end, becomes a source of blessing.

In prayer, we may have to wrestle with God. We read in Genesis 32 that Jacob wrestled with him and limped for ever afterwards. It is not wrong to ask God questions. We will not get immediate answers. Personally, I find it often takes quite a long time before I see what I am looking for. The answer may come in something someone says, or I may read it in a book, or an idea comes into my mind. God does speak to us but not in voices from heaven, at least I do not hear him that way. Prayer is a relationship and if you treat it as such, you will find God does teach you. You will learn about God, gain new insights, find answers to difficult questions, and gradually you will find you are beginning to know something of this God of ours, who can come to us in powerful storms or great winds or in gentle breezes, 'who visits us like the dawn from on high' (from the Benedictus).

FOR REFLECTION

1. What is your reaction when you see Jesus being scourged, ill treated, and crucified and he does not defend himself?

2. Can you accept God when he does not show signs that he is present and he allows his creatures to all but prove that he does not exist.

3. Which do you prefer, the God who came down at Elijah's bidding and consummed the sacrifice with fire (see 1 Kings 18:20–40) or the God who waits patiently and refuses to blow people's minds?

4. Have you ever felt helpless in trying to tell others about God? Did this discourage you or could you find strength in your weakness?

PRAYER

Lord, you are certainly not like us. Even my best ideas of you are not you. How can I know you unless you come and teach me yourself. You have sent me your Holy Spirit to do just that. Spirit of the living God I ask you to show me the Lord. Grant to me an understanding that does not come from reasoning, just show me the Lord. Amen.

Praying through the Spirit

◆——————◆

IMAGINE a very small island, set far out in the Pacific Ocean, a long way from any land mass or other island, lying somewhere between latitude 20 and 30 degrees south of the equator. At most its length would be just over 3 miles and at its widest it is just under 1 mile. The island is very rocky and that could explain why humans never seem to have settled there. When I say it is rocky. I do not mean you to imagine a solid rock mass, bare and forbidding in the hot sun, rather it is covered in rocky outcrops, and soil between the rocks is poor and does not go very deep. In this soil all sorts of plants grow and many of them have beautiful flowers. At the north end of the island, where the widest part lies, there are a few trees.

The island supports a number of animals and insects. You can find lizards, snakes, rodents, and of course many birds. The main inhabitant is the turtle. Rather strange to say, there are butterflies on the island, but for some unknown reason they have never learnt to fly. They have wings, in fact they are quite large and they are of beautiful colours. Often you will see them sitting on the rocks displaying these iridescent colours to any who would care to admire them. But, while these butterflies may be very beautiful, life is not that easy for them. When they climb up the stalks of the flowers to get at the nectar and pollen, the great sails on their backs become quite a problem, especially when the plants are growing close together. The real difficulty starts when they try to come down. They have to come down backwards and this means that the wings get hopelessly entangled with awkward stems criss-crossing in the mass of vegetation. But, then, life has its problems, and so they have learnt to live with them.

One day there was an immense storm and every living thing had to seek shelter somewhere on the island. Under every rock and stone, you could have found some small, or not so small, creature sheltering for its life. The wind blew, and the rain came down in buckets and it lasted for most of the day. When finally it had blown itself out and the sun came out to dry up the soaked island, all the small creatures came out to see what was left of their homes.

Soon news travelled round that something interesting had been found. In the north part of the island there was a very drenched butterfly, obviously blown there from some far off land, and the exciting thing was that this butterfly could fly.

It was Tommy Toad who found her. He knew straight away that she was not from the island, for her wings were rather shabby and were not highly coloured as the other butterflies.

'How have you come here? I do not recall ever seeing you before.'

'I was flying when a great storm arose and before I could get to my home I was blown out to sea. From then on I do not remember much until I opened my eyes not long ago. Can you tell me where I am?', she said rather sadly.

'You are not far from Turtle Cove,' Tommy replied, 'but what is all this about flying? Here the butterflies do not fly.'

'They don't fly', she answered incredulously. 'But

that is what wings are for.' And she opened her wings to allow the sun to dry them. After a few moments she flew up into the air to demonstrate to Tommy who sat there with his eyes bulging with astonishment.

'Wait here', said Tommy and he rushed off to assemble as many of the island's butterflies as he could find.

It did not take very long to gather a large crowd for the island was small and news travelled quickly. Tommy addressed the assembled crowd and was obviously very proud of his find. After the necessary introductions the little butterfly demonstrated the art of flying while the crowd gasped and ooed.

'So that's what they are for. Why didn't someone tell us?' The excitement was intense and some of the younger butterflies immediately began to try their skill at flying, but not having very strong muscles, nor being well versed in aeronautics, there were accidents. The older and so-called wiser ones, went round the island shaking their heads saying: 'It is all very dangerous.'

◆━━━━◆

There are many different gifts, but it is always the same Spirit; there are many different ways of serving, but it is always the same Lord. There are many different forms of activity, but in everybody it is the same God who is at work in them all. The particular manifestation of the Spirit granted to each one is to be used for the general good. To one is given from the Spirit the gift of utterance expressing wisdom; to another the gift of utterance expressing knowledge, in accordance with the same Spirit; to another, faith, from the same Spirit; and to another, the gifts of healing, through this one Spirit; to another, the working of miracles; to another, prophecy; to another, the power of distinguishing spirits; to one, the gift of different tongues and to another, the interpretation of tongues. But at

work in all these is one and the same Spirit, distribut-
ing them at will to each individual.

(1 Corinthians 12:4–11)

When I studied theology, we cannot have spent much time on the gifts of the Holy Spirit because I cannot recall anything about them. The general opinion at that time seemed to be that these gifts were only given to the Church at the beginning so, as it were, to give it a boost.

Since Vatican II we know that this is not the case. In the Document on the Church (section 12) it says that the gifts of the Holy Spirit belong to the whole Church, they are not reserved for the clergy alone, and they are to be received with gratitude. In the passage from 1 Corinthians, Paul lists the gifts of the Spirit; we are not concerned with them all here, but there are books written which deal specifically with them, or there are wise people in the church who can help us explore them further.

Rather like the butterflies who had never used their wings, we, who have never been instructed in the gifts, have not known quite how to allow them to operate. Mistakes have been made, and, sadly, the charisms (as they are sometimes called) are now often viewed with suspicion.

The gifts of the Holy Spirit belong to the Holy Spirit and can be lent to any believer 'for the general good' (1 Corinthians 12:7). They are gifts for service and any member of the church can be used by the Holy Spirit for the Spirit's purpose. It is wrong to think that these gifts are only confined to people in the charismatic renewal. The object of the renewal is precisely to restore the gifts to the whole church.

So what about praying in the Spirit? How can we let the Spirit speak to us? I think it is helpful to see human

beings in terms of body, soul and spirit (although, of
course, we should be a little wary of categorising things
too simply). Through the body we are 'physical' beings
and partake in the material world. Through the soul
we are 'rational' beings, able to live in the immaterial
as well as the material world and bringing into play our
reason, our will, our imagination and our emotions.
Through the spirit we are 'spiritual' beings and operate
in a realm beyond the reach of body and soul. It is
through our spirit that God communicates with us by
his Spirit. 'The Spirit himself joins with our spirit to
bear witness that we are children of God' (Romans
8:16).

We can learn about God through our intellects. We
are taught the truths about God, but these truths can
be just information, facts; they need to become bearers
of life. This is the work of the Holy Spirit. He can take
what we learn through our minds and make it life-
giving or he can impart life-giving knowledge directly
through our spirits into our minds – this we call inspiration. God promised that he would lead us into truth
this way.

> but the Paraclete, the Holy Spirit,
> whom the Father will send in my name,
> will teach you everything
> and remind you of all I have said to you.
>
> (John 14:26)

In the western world we rely heavily on receiving
knowledge through our reason and intellect. We are
logical, scientific. In our times, the Holy Spirit is being
rediscovered, but many of us are in danger of being too
cerebral; we are suspicious of inspiration, of dreams,
of inner enlightenments. I believe it is right for the
Church to be cautious about inner promptings as there
are plenty of nutcases around who imagine every
prompting must be the Holy Spirit. Satan can manifest

himself as an angel of light, and care must be taken
that we are not led astray. What we most need is
discernment (referred to in Paul's list as the 'power of
distinguishing spirits'). We need to discern which spirit
is at work – the Holy Spirit, the human spirit or an
evil spirit?

When we pray we can use our bodies to help us.
Posture and gestures can both be employed. We can
use our imaginations, our minds, our memories. But
God can also use our spirits, and when he does so,
he bypasses our body and reasoning process, and goes
directly to our spirit. We cannot cause this to happen
– it is God's work and he knows when to do it. I see
this as the beginning of contemplation. I don't think
contemplation is about having great illuminations or
visions or hearing voices. It seems at first to be a
great darkness for God is not communicating with us
through our reason but through our spirit. It is God's
gift to us and hence not something we should actively
seek.

The gifts of the Spirit that St Paul writes about also
operate in this realm of the spirit. I believe much teaching is needed about these gifts if they are to be used
rightly. One of the gifts mentioned is that of wisdom,
and an example of this is when we receive insights
from God to help us in a given situation – perhaps to
help us counsel another person. We seem to receive
from beyond ourselves the right words to say, or perhaps we receive a particular insight which gives us
new understanding.

I don't think the gift of tongues (the last on Paul's
list) is such a weird gift as many people imagine. We
have had very little teaching about it in the Catholic
Church and perhaps that explains the mystery surrounding it. I am sure we all recognise that there are
times in prayer when we simply do not have the words
to express ourselves. It could be a time of great conso-

lation or desolation – both experiences can reduce us
to silence. The gift of tongues operates when the Holy
Spirit begins to pray through people. Unintelligible
words, what seems like a foreign language, sounds
with no apparent meaning come out, but I believe that
at a deeper level this prayer does have meaning even
if our minds cannot grasp it. 'The Spirit too comes to
help us in our weakness, for, when we do not know
how to pray properly, then the Spirit personally makes
our petitions for us in groans that cannot be put into
words; and he who sees into all hearts knows what
the Spirit means because the prayers that the Spirit
makes for God's holy people are always in accordance
with the mind of God.' (Romans 8:26,27)

As I say, this is a complex area and one that needs
much more exploration than I can give here. If we are
going to take prayer seriously, we will need to find a
wise guide to help us move into the realm of praying
in the Spirit.

FOR REFLECTION

1. When you pray, who do you talk to? The Father,
   Jesus or the Holy Spirit?
2. Why do you think the Holy Spirit gets neglected?
3. Do you know the difference between the gifts of
   the Holy Spirit and the fruit of the Holy Spirit? (See
   1 Corinthians 12:4–11 and Galatians 5:22–26.)
4. We have received the Holy Spirit in many different
   ways, so we can all say 'we have got the Holy Spirit'.
   The real question is 'Has the Holy Spirit got us?'
   Has he got you?

PRAYER

Holy Spirit of God. Forgive me for neglecting you so
often. You are the one who always talks about the

Father and Jesus. Please talk to me about them so that I begin to know them and not just know about them. You were sent to me for this very reason; please, I invite you to teach me. Amen.

Two Ways of Asking

◄════►

Eleanor's heart sank when she saw from her notebook that number 27 Snellgrove Road was her next port of call. Eleanor was a home help, and Eileen Grindmore, to whom she was now going, was a very demanding person. Eileen was confined to a wheelchair, and had been for some years, but she always had long lists of requests when Eleanor went to visit. Eleanor found the constant demands quite exhausting.

'I've been waiting for you all morning', were the words that greeted Eleanor as she entered the house with a somewhat heavy heart. 'I want you to pop down to the corner shop and get me some string, some ribbons, and some Christmas wrapping paper. We've got to get these presents wrapped and ready, for there is now not much time left.'

'I also want some bread, and would you look and see if there is any fruit in the larder? I shall also want you to phone Mrs Rye and ask her to be sure that she calls in here after she has collected her daughter from school.' And so it went on, one request after another. Eleanor knew that poor Mrs Grindmore was severely handicapped and that she depended upon someone to help her, but in some way Eleanor felt she was just an object to be used.

Annie Punch was very different. She was also handicapped and confined to a wheelchair, but, somehow

Eleanor, though she would work just as hard for her, looked forward to those visits. On arrival Eleanor would be made to sit down and tell Mrs Punch all that had happened since her last visit. She wanted to know everything and she seemed to have a very good memory, and remembered to ask about this and that. It was only in the course of conversation that requests would appear. 'I've bought a few Christmas presents and I have tried parcelling them up, and they look a real mess, I wonder . . .' and she would give that rather helpless look which said, 'I really am not much use, and it pains me to be like that. Forgive me for needing someone like you.' Those words were not said, but what was communicated was, 'I cannot do it, but that is how things are and I accept them'. Of course, Eleanor was only too delighted to take the crinkled heap that was on the table and unwrap it, straighten out the paper and make a new parcel.

Eleanor often wondered what the difference was between these two handicapped people. Maybe it was that Mrs Punch rarely asked for anything just for herself; and yet Mrs Grindmore also had parcels for other people. Was it the way in which Mrs Punch asked that was so different? Mrs Grindmore seemed to be giving orders, whereas Mrs Punch seemed to make the request out of her helplessness, and yet there was no sense of seeking pity or sympathy.

'That is why I am telling you not to worry about your life and what you are to eat, nor about your body and what you are to wear. Surely life is more than food, and the body more than clothing! Look at the birds in the sky. They do not sow or reap or gather into barns; yet your heavenly Father feeds them. Are you not worth much more than they are! Can any of you, however much you worry, add one single cubit to your

*span of life? And why worry about clothing? Think of
the flowers growing in the fields; they never have to
work or spin; yet I assure you that not even Solomon
in all his royal robes was clothed like one of these.
Now if that is how God clothes the wild flowers growing in the field which are there today and thrown into
the furnace tomorrow, will he not much more look
after you, you who have so little faith? So do not
worry; do not say, "What are we to eat? What are we
to drink? What are we to wear?" It is the gentiles who
set their hearts on all these things. Your heavenly
Father knows you need them all. Set your hearts on
his kingdom first, and on God's saving justice, and all
these other things will be given you as well. So do not
worry about tomorrow: tomorrow will take care of
itself. Each day has enough trouble of its own.'*

(Matthew 6:25–34)

I imagine that most of us learnt about prayer as asking
God for our needs. We ask him to bless our mother
and father, our brothers and sisters. We also thank him
for the good things we have received and ask for his
protection. I can remember tacking onto the family
list, friends and relatives until the list became a long
litany. I had dreadful problems pruning it. I felt guilty
if I left someone out and feared some terrible thing
would happen to them. What odd creatures we are. I
know someone who for years prayed for 'the woman
who fell out of the train'. He had read this in the paper
and had felt compassion for the poor soul, so she got
tucked into the family list. We can learn to rattle
through these lists without paying attention, and my
friend told me that years after reading about this poor
woman, he discovered that he was still mentioning
her in his automatic list.

Many of us need to realise that there is much more

to prayer than petition. In the passage from Matthew, God is asking us what our priorities are. Are we too concerned with our own wants and wishes? Jesus tells us that if we spent more time seeking the kingdom of God, then many of our requests would actually get attended to without us bothering about them. But what does it mean to seek the kingdom of God? Many people think that the kingdom of God refers to heaven, but if this is so, how can we seek the kingdom through prayer?

I think, instead, we should see the kingdom of God as wherever God is obeyed, wherever God is accepted to be in charge. To seek the kingdom of God is to search into our lives and see if we are allowing God to have his way.

To obey God is to accept his Son. Most of us would think that to obey God means following his commandments. While, this is of course true, the following of God's commandments comes second to accepting the gift of his Son. In John's Gospel, Jesus tells us what obeying the Father means: 'This is carrying out God's work: you must believe in the one he has sent.' (John 6:29)

So, when we pray we need to acknowledge to the Father that we believe in and accept his son. We thank him for this wonderful gift, we ask his pardon that we did not accept Jesus when he lived on earth, but hounded him out of the city and hung him on a cross. We bless the Father for taking this terrible act of ours and using it for his purposes. Time and time again we tell the Father that we accept all that he has done for us in his son. We thank him that through Christ, sins are forgiven, that we can live a new life as God's children. This is to seek the kingdom of God. We ask that what the Father has achieved may have its full effect in us and in the world.

Many of the prayers said in church express all these

truths, but because these truths have not yet become ours we can tend to mouth the words and not grasp the full meaning. For example, we can call our Lord our saviour, but do we act as though he is our saviour? Say, for example, that we were told that we would be dead next week, where would we put our hope? Would it be in a list of good things we have done? Or would we immediately say: 'My hope and trust are in the merits of Jesus Christ'?

So how do we see prayer? Do we view it as a series of requests we present to God? As a list of people we have promised to pray for? Or, as in Eleanor's relationship with Mrs Punch, is it more of a conversation, a real relating? The Scripture passage is showing us that petitions should not be our priority in prayer. Naturally, we want to tell God our needs but there is something wrong if they dominate the relationship. There is much more to life and to prayer than petition and worrying about our own wants and wishes. The passage is not telling us just to sit around expecting God to feed and clothe us. The Lord is saying, 'Seek the kingdom first, and then attend to your needs'. To seek the kingdom is to want Jesus Christ to take his rightful place as Lord and master of this earth. He himself told us that all power and all authority had been given to him; we invite him to exercise that power and authority, beginning in our own lives.

FOR REFLECTION

1. What are your priorities in prayer? Do petitions dominate?
2. If they do dominate, what does that show about your image of God?
3. What do you think it means to 'set your heart on the kingdom first'? How might that affect your own life and the way you pray?

PRAYER

Father God you know my needs and you know how much they mean to me. Do not let me become so immersed in my wants that I forget your wants. I thank you that you are loving and you know and understand how things are with me. Teach me about your kingdom, heal me of my blindness. May your Spirit teach me that I belong to you and you belong to me. Thank you for being you. Amen.

Unanswered Prayer

HIS NAME IS XU GUOMING. I have no idea how one pronounces it, and that has proved a problem because I undertook to pray for him.

I first saw his photo on the front page of a newspaper. Beside the photo, in large letters, was the heading:

FIRST PROTESTERS SENTENCED TO DEATH IN CHINA.

My friend, and I feel I can now call him that, looked so young and alone, and I suppose it was just that which caught my mind – or was it my heart? It was a head and shoulders photo, and although his head was slightly bowed, his eyes were raised and looking straight in front of him. Whether he was looking at the person reading his death sentence, I do not know, but I do know that the drama of that moment was communicated to me. On his left was the face of a soldier, also young, but the peak of his military cap was pulled well down over his face and all that I could see was his mouth, which was stern and set.

I wondered what it must be like to hear a sentence of death being passed on you. I could imagine my own fear and panic, and I wanted to stretch out to this unknown stranger from the other side of the world. It was then that I undertook to pray for him.

I cut the photo out and pasted it on my cupboard

door to make sure that I would not forget him. I felt a bit ashamed at doing this. Surely I would remember this young man and his trouble without having to put his picture on my door? But I went ahead and his picture is still there.

I prayed and prayed that God would spare him from the sentence passed. I prayed anywhere I could – while shopping, as I walked from one place to another. I was somewhat encouraged when after a few days I read in the papers that various heads of government had sent messages asking for leniency. I was hopeful that these requests might be listened to.

It must have been ten days after first noticing his picture in the papers, that I saw on television that the death sentence had been carried out. I was watching the news one evening and they announced that three young people had been executed, and I saw some shots taken of the three men being marched into a vast public hall to be executed in front of a large, silent crowd. Thank God we were spared seeing the execution, but I did see my friend just for a moment and that picture still haunts me. I can remember trying to comfort myself by saying: 'Well, he is dead now. He does not have to fear it anymore. It is over.' All I could do now was to commend him to God.

Had my prayers failed? Did I not pray enough? Should I have asked others to pray? Did God not hear me? Why should he hear me, a westerner, someone living a comfortable and maybe compromised life? A veritable storm was let loose in me and all sorts of frightening questions burst into my mind.

━━━◆━━━

'So I say to you: *Ask, and it will be given to you; search, and you will find; knock, and the door will be opened to you. For everyone who asks receives; everyone who searches finds; everyone who knocks*

will have the door opened. What father among you, if
his son asked for a fish would hand him a snake? Or
if he asked for an egg, hand him a scorpion? If you
then, evil as you are, know how to give your children
what is good, how much more will the heavenly
Father give the Holy Spirit to those who ask him!'

(Luke 11:9–13)

What does this passage from St Luke mean? Is it really
saying that God will grant all our requests? Why then
did my young Chinese friend die when I was praying
so hard for him? I don't know the answer to that question, but I do know that many of us, myself included,
have faulty pictures of God and we need to let these
be changed in the light of Jesus' life, death and resurrection. Perhaps we will then see that God's purposes are
different from ours and that we need to trust him
more. Perhaps we will see that he *does* answer our
prayers, but in ways we would not expect or cannot
fully understand in this life. If, as Jesus says in the
above passage, God gives good things to his children,
mustn't it be true that God's ways are more than we
can comprehend and our images of him are often inadequate?

My own pictures of God have undergone, and are
still undergoing, transformation. I grew up understanding him to be almighty and powerful, I imagined that
he conquered evil by blowing it out of existence by
force. Over quite a number of years now I have begun
to understand that God often seems to deal with evil
through apparent weakness. When Jesus started his
public life, he did miracles, cured the sick, raised the
dead. In other words he seemed to come against Satan
with power and strength. But after the transfiguration
he seemed to change. He now talked about going to
Jerusalem and dying.

On Mount Tabor, Moses and Elijah appeared with him and we are told that they were talking about 'his passing'. Was Jesus then receiving clearer instruction from his Father about the Father's way of defeating Satan? After this encounter on the mount, Jesus was different. He did fewer miracles and he set his face like flint to go to Jerusalem. He began to refer more and more to his death and resurrection, and his disciples did not know what he was talking about.

Jesus could have conquered Satan at a moment's notice, but it seemed the Father was going to defeat Satan by apparently allowing him to conquer his Son. Jesus permitted the evil one to do his damnedest against him. But having died, having allowed the worst to happen, Jesus was called back by the Father from the kingdom of darkness and thus through weakness Jesus overcame. He calls us to follow him. It seems that he is asking us to trust that he can turn even what appears to us a disaster into something from which good can come. He is our Father, he loves us and wants the best for us. Who can tell how he used my prayers, and no doubt the prayers of many others, for some good purpose? True, the young man died, but life here on earth is not our final aim.

I believe God to be good and I feel content to allow my friend to fall into his hands. At Mass we pray for the departed and after mentioning our 'brothers and sisters', meaning all Christians no matter what denomination, we add 'and all those who have left this world in your friendship'. That is a fairly wide-ranging prayer. Many people may well be in God's friendship without actually knowing God personally. This does not mean that I deny that no one can come to the Father save through Jesus Christ; it is still through Christ that we all go to the Father, but God is the judge and not us. That is why I love the Church's care for everyone, no matter who they are.

If we judge things according to this life alone, we will find many things to lament and regret. But we need to remember that we were not made just for this life. Our prayers may seem unanswered now but we do not always see things as God sees them, and much of the Christian journey is about learning to trust him even when things look desperate and he appears to have abandoned us.

FOR REFLECTION

1. How do you judge things? Is it from the viewpoint of this life or from the viewpoint of eternity?
2. How do you react to upsets in life and to times when your prayers seem to go unanswered?
3. What are the things that you pray about?
4. Can you really trust God?

PRAYER

Lord, from where I stand I see many needs and wants. You have promised that if we ask you would answer.

I do find it very difficult to see how you answer some of my prayers. I know you are not bound to answer my prayers in the way I would like you to do, but at times it really does look as though you did not hear me.

Forgive me for talking to you in this way, but I want you to be a God I can say anything to. Thank you for not being touchy. I offer you my mind and ask you to enlighten me. I am sure that is what you want. Amen.

When Prayer becomes Difficult

 ⟵━━━▶

IT WAS SOME YEARS now since Ronald had made the retreat that so changed his life. Jane, his wife, had suggested that as the family were all but off their hands, they should go for the last few days of Holy Week to an abbey not too far from where they lived. Ronald, who would not have called himself a religious type, though he had remained loyal to the practice of his faith, thought the idea was good and it seemed a fine thing to do.

There was nothing very outstanding about the retreat, most of the participants thought it was helpful, nice, pleasant, but for Ronald it was life changing. Truths, which he had known and thought he had accepted, suddenly took on a new and staggering meaning. Quite simply, Ronald had met God in all his wonder, mercy and love. The outcome of the retreat was that Ronald began to read Scripture and to pray. He decided to give up a quarter of an hour of his lunch break and spent it in a church quite close to his office in the heart of the city.

Prayer, became a new experience. Before he had mumbled prayers asking God to bless his family, his work, and, in times of tension or crisis, he allowed this prayer time to be lengthened a little. He could see that there was quite a lot of self in those prayers, everything was rather geared to what he wanted and God was seen as the 'wealthy one' who could provide if stroked nicely. He could even see quite a bit of superstition in the way he used to think. What held him now was the fact that God was good. He did not have to win his favour. The incredible thing was that God loved Ronald, he loved everyone and he wanted to be loved in return. Ronald found that his prayer became God centred, God was no longer seen for what he could do for Ronald. What had seized hold of Ronald's mind was that before he had made any response to God's love, God had sent his Son to die for his sins and had risen from death and wanted to live in Ronald and help him live for God and not for himself. This fact bowled Ronald over; it was not a calculating love, it was not tit for tat, it was totally generous.

For several months after that retreat during his prayer time he kept coming back to these truths, which he had listened to many times, but somehow had not really heard. He pondered over them and never seemed to tire of them.

Soon questions began to rise up from all this pondering and these led him to books. There were some at the back of the church where he prayed, but they were few in number. He noticed a small notice giving the address of the shop that supplied them. He now began to buy books and to read. He found that he was really quite ignorant about the truths of his faith. The problem he found in the book shop was that there were so many books and they all seemed to be exactly what he ought to read, though he soon discovered that not all of them lived up to their promise. Fortunately, Mr Dart, who served in the shop, was widely read and his advice proved of immense help.

But all this was, as it were, in the past. Ronald was now beginning to experience this time of prayer as burdensome. He certainly was not so faithful to the fifteen minutes and at the least provocation he was ready to arrive late or go early. Somehow the time had lost its freshness and the ideas, which had so held his mind, no longer had their appeal. Also he was full of distractions and it seemed as if God had gone away, and the fifteen minutes, once not long enough, now seemed interminable. The temptation was to skip this time of prayer. He was getting nothing from it, in fact he seemed to become more and more irritable, clearly it was no good going on flogging a dead horse. He also found that the books he had turned to had lost their interest, and the train journey home was now spent with the evening paper.

This state of things went on for some time, and while Ronald did make some gallant efforts to keep up his prayer, he felt he was fighting a losing battle, then one day when he went to the church during his lunch hour he found a mission was in progress. He had only just walked in when he heard the priest say: 'When you no longer get anything out of prayer, you are on the brink of learning how to pray'. Ronald made enquiries and found out who the priest was and he made an appointment with him. Ronald had found a spiritual director who could begin to explain to him just what was happening in his spiritual life.

Now when I came to you, brothers, I did not come with any brilliance of oratory or wise argument to announce to you the mystery of God. I was resolved that the only knowledge I would have while I was with you was knowledge of Jesus, and of him as the crucified Christ. I came among you in weakness, in fear and great trembling and what I spoke and proclaimed was not meant to convince by philosophical argument, but to demonstrate the convincing power

*of the Spirit, so that your faith should depend not on
human wisdom but on the power of God ... Now,
the Spirit we have received is not the spirit of the
world, but God's own Spirit, so that we may understand the lavish gifts God has given us. And these are
what we speak of, not in the terms learnt from human
philosophy, but in terms learnt from the Spirit, fitting
spiritual language to spiritual things.*

(1 Corinthians 2:1–5, 12–13)

I once had to go to a foot therapy class. We were
told to open and close our toes and to waggle them
independently of each other. My toes are like soldiers,
whatever the big toe does the rest follow in military
obedience. I complained to the therapist that it was
impossible for me to do what she was asking. She
simply replied: 'You have got the muscles, therefore
you can learn to use them.'

As we saw in the chapter on 'Praying through the
Spirit' every person has a spirit, but since we are not
able to see it, feel it, sense it, we tend to neglect it and
we pay much more attention to our bodies and minds.
If we neglect to use our spirit, then it, like muscles,
becomes all but paralysed. The Holy Spirit contacts us
through our spirit, but if we are out of touch with our
spirit, then we successfully block the Holy Spirit.

We can learn about God through our minds. We can
be taught truths about God. We can learn that he
created the world, he sent his Son to save us, he did
this through the cross and resurrection. But these
truths can just remain facts learnt but not life giving.
It is the Spirit of God that has to take these truths
and through his revelation to our spirit bring life to
something that could just remain an intellectual truth.

Ronald, in the story, experienced the Holy Spirit
illuminating truths that he already knew – but until

then it had just been a bit of knowledge, not something life giving. It was a gift of God to Ronald when he burst in to his life during that retreat. What was important, was that Ronald took this gift and began to work at it, developing it and letting it grow.

God deals with each of us as individuals and he knows how best to approach us. He drops us lots of little hints, which alas, we are often very lazy about. Sometimes he has, as it were, to shout to catch our attention. We can even abuse this and just enjoy the sudden flood of insights, but fundamentally remain unchanged. Ronald responded and so Ronald grew.

When Ronald found prayer becoming difficult, this was God again beginning to act. Everyone of us is born self-centred and even after God has awakened us and made us aware of him, we can still follow him for very selfish reasons. All that has happened is that our objective has changed – once it was material things, now it is spiritual – but self is still in the driving seat. God, in his own time, knows when to start correcting us. This cannot be rushed, we cannot cause it to happen – try being forgetful of self and you will soon see the problem.

The way God has to do it is to make us aware of our poverty, our shallowness, our sinfulness. When prayer becomes difficult, God is asking us 'Are you here for me or for you?' If we give up prayer because we no longer 'get anything out of it' then clearly we were praying for self-centred reasons. The whole prayer experience is a journey into God away from self. Our very way of being is to be centred on ourself. We see everything from where we are; we cannot even begin to imagine what it looks like from where God is, until God begins to show us. This is a moment of crisis and many who meet it give up praying and become busy affirming themselves, doing something they can claim credit for.

God made us for himself. Therefore the self is good. But we stole the self from God and made it into ego. We said 'I want me for me' and we live in the illusion that one day we will find total satisfaction in the 'me'. There is no escape from this prison, until we allow the one who became a man and never lived for the 'me' to set us free. 'Unless a wheat grain falls into the earth and dies, it remains only a single grain' (John 12:24). There has to come a dying and it is not a dying that we arrange. We can practise great self-effacement, we can learn to sit in the lowest seat, but the ego can flourish on such a diet. It is only when Jesus calls us into the fire of the cross, can he cause death and resurrection.

Let's face it, a prayer life can be sought after because we think that will put us among the special ones. We must remember that 'Blessed are the poor in spirit' – we are blessed when we fail, when we cannot pray, when we see the sin within ourselves, when we have nothing to boast of save that he who fashioned rainbows also made us and can and will refashion us in his time. Maybe he is delaying that refashioning until we, having died, will not take any of his glory for ourselves.

FOR REFLECTION

1. Do you judge your prayer by how much you get out of it?
2. What do you do when prayer becomes dry? Examine your conscience? Slog on? Review your ways of praying?
3. Are you content simply to be in his presence? This does not mean necessarily that you will feel it, but are you content just to know he is there?

PRAYER

Lord, no thought or idea I have ever had of you, is you. You are greater than any thought of mine could ever dream up. I want, not thoughts of you, I want you. Come! Yet, as I say that I know you have come. Amen.

Praying through the Church

←——→

AN AMERICAN WOMAN is reported to have said: 'Sure, I love God, but I'm not nuts about him.' Most of us, I am sure, know only too well what she means, but we would not have put it quite in that way.

We live in a world where every form of experience is now available and I wonder if our senses have become over stimulated, over-fed, so that they can no longer be satisfied with the normal and people are ever on the look out for something new, something more powerful. 'I'm bored, what's new' is a cry often heard. Clearly to keep up with this demand is going to prove ever more impossible, for we cannot go on finding new sensations and experiences.

My prayer life started, as most people's, with seeing prayer as asking God for my wants and needs. Even when I prayed the rosary, I was saying these prayers for an intention and I was not doing as I should, pondering all that Christ had done for my salvation. I was just saying some Our Fathers many Hail Marys and a few Glory bes, in the hope that many prayers would get a better hearing.

School retreats, with their imposed silences, did leave me with questions as to how to occupy the silence. Clearly one could not fill them with endless petitions. I think most of us solved this problem by reading lives of saints. I remember one book I read was about a young French boy who had visions of Our Lady. This set me longing for a vision and I remember going into the church one night after supper when all was dark. I settled myself in the Lady Chapel to await my vision. I do not remember what I said while I waited. In the church there was an old organ and before anyone played it its power had to be turned on. This would sound like the rushing of a great wind. Unknown to me someone came into the church to practise the organ, and when I heard the mighty wind, I was out of that church before you could have said 'Holy Smoke', and away down the school passage like a scalded cat. So much for my vision.

I am amazed now at my ignorance of the basic Christian truths. I do not blame anyone for this ignorance, because I have been a teacher and I know how people can just not hear you. My idea of God was more of a disciplinarian than a loving father. I can see quite easily how a person could pick up such an idea. The trouble is that once an idea has come to rest, all other ideas can be coloured by it.

Prayers in church went over my head. I was not praying prayers of thanksgiving, I was not adoring God for the gift of his Son, I was not asking that his death and resurrection should affect my life. I was asking for favours, so nothing I heard in church touched my world.

In those days the Mass was in Latin and that did not help. It is true I had a missal, and I learnt to follow in English, but even the English was not my everyday language – it all seemed so foreign. So no wonder I was bored and alas, I expected to be bored, because God did not seem to appear in my life or even be a bit interested in it.

◆━━━━◆

'Be careful not to forget Yahweh your God, by neglecting his commandments, customs and laws which I
am laying down for you today. When you have eaten
all you want, when you have built fine houses to live
in, when you have seen your flocks and herds increase,
your silver and gold abound and all your possessions
grow great, do not become proud of heart. Do not
then forget Yahweh your God who brought you out of
Egypt, out of the place of slave-labour, who guided
you through this vast and dreadful desert, a land of
fiery snakes, scorpions, thirst; who in this waterless
place brought you water out of the flinty rock; who
in this desert fed you with manna unknown to your
ancestors, to humble you and test you and so make
your future the happier.

'Beware of thinking to yourself, "My own strength
and the might of my own hand have given me the
power to act like this." Remember Yahweh your God;
he was the one who gave you the strength to act
effectively like this, thus keeping then, as today, the
covenant which he swore to your ancestors. Be sure:
if you forget Yahweh your God, if you follow other
gods, if you serve them and bow down to them – I
testify to you today – you will perish. Like the nations
Yahweh is to destroy before you, so you yourselves
will perish, for not having listened to the voice of
Yahweh your God.'

(Deuteronomy 8:11–20)

◆━━━━◆

Church is not theatre, and just as the Jews had an
obligation to teach their sons the meaning behind the
family ceremonies celebrated each Sabbath, so Christians need to educate their children in what Church
ceremonies stand for. If we have not been grounded in

the fact that Jesus stood in for us when he died then we will wonder why the Church constantly talks about the death of Christ. We may find it morbid, rather depressing, could even get guilty feelings about it; but once we have seen the love that drove Jesus to accept suffering in our place, we will find that it becomes an event we do not want to forget. But Jesus did more than die in our place, he rose up from the dead and has become the new Adam and he wants us to allow him to live in us thus enabling us to live in a new way.

The Church is God's instrument whereby he continues to care for us. It is made up of fallible people, through whom the Holy Spirit brings to perfection all that Jesus achieved for us through his death and resurrection. In the course of the year the Church calls to mind the great events whereby Christ won eternal life for us. Before Christmas we wait as the chosen people waited all those centuries for the promised Messiah. This sense of expectancy reminds us that Jesus is coming again. We are urged to long for his return, not so that our troubles will be over, but so that the great work of Jesus will be completed. He will receive due honour and glory. Many of us have quite a long way to grow before we can honestly say we look forward to heaven, not as a place where we will be totally happy, but as a place where God's plans will have been totally fulfilled.

At Christmas, we ponder the mystery how God became man. We will never be able to fathom this mystery. How can he who is everywhere be suddenly confined to somewhere? How can he who is all powerful be suddenly limited? How can he who knows everything ever learn?

During Lent, Easter and Pentecost we continue to ponder the mystery of Christ dying and rising from the dead. We try and grasp the evil of sin, we celebrate our reconciliation with the Father and praise God for the sending of his Holy Spirit.

In doing this the Church is teaching us how to pray. Prayer is more than petition, it is the praising of God for his mighty being, his marvellous creation and his saving power. Every time we call to mind what God has done for us, we are affected more and more deeply by that saving event. To help us pray the Church puts Scripture before us where we hear what God has done, and then puts psalms on our lips so that we respond to these great acts of God. Praying with the Church is not just saying prayers, it is praying with meaning the prayers that are spoken during services. Signs and symbols are used to illustrate meanings more deeply. Music and songs are used to help us worship God.

FOR REFLECTION

1. In our personal prayer time, do we do as the Church does when it prays?
2. Do you find the prayers the Church puts on our lips often express very well the sentiments that are in our hearts?
3. Is your spiritual life very personal and private? Do you object to others being with you at Mass?

PRAYER

Jesus, I thank you for your church. I thank you for the wisdom you have given her ever since you founded her. I bless you for the way you have shaped her through pain, questionings, open rebellion and persecution. Help me to learn through her wisdom. Teach me to listen to all that she has learnt. I thank you for the many whose lives have enriched her understanding. Give me a love for your Church. Never let me be a cause for her blushing. Amen.

Praying through the Word

It is quite easy to see now how I grew up fearing God. I learned that he was good, that he wanted me to be good; I was told that he was almighty and therefore could do anything he wished. I also learnt that he could be angry, that he caused the flood, sent fiery serpents among his people when they made a golden calf to be worshipped. In my mind's eye I can still see some of the horrific pictures in the book we had of Old Testament stories depicting these terrible events. So, all in all, I learnt many conflicting truths about God, and that made him very confusing and mysterious.

I suppose what affected me most was the way I experienced God. Since he was good and almighty I asked him for favours. I would ask for a variety of things. For picnics and days out I would ask for fine weather. Exams always seemed to be looming and that would get me to lengthen my prayers. In our family I heard of troubles and problems afflicting relatives, so prayers for their intentions were said. Life has many difficulties and so all these intentions, plus deliverance from school terms, were put before this all powerful God. Not many of my prayers seemed to get answered, so in my boyish heart, I came to the conclusion that if this God is almighty and he does not use his mighty

power to help me, then I cannot figure very high in
his estimation.

I now see a sharp distinction between what I learnt
about God and how I experienced him. No matter how
another person is described to you, if you experience
them differently, then that counts far more than what
anyone says. I feel this is significant for it explains to
me how I could not take in the positive teachings that
I must have heard.

Our minds become set and it takes a long time and
much effort before they can be shifted. I do not think
I would have admitted to having a fear of God for it is
quite possible to have an attitude and be quite blind
to it. My life was not evil, I went to church, I practised
the gospel reasonably well, I said my prayers and was
a respectable citizen. So I did not see how things really
were in my life, and that I had a fear of God.

Today, even after understanding something of this
problem, I can still react in situations of tension with
feelings of resentment against God. For instance, I hate
rushing to be on time. I like to leave myself plenty of
leeway. Thus if trains are late, or traffic is heavy, I
become tense. I find myself saying: 'Come on Lord,
get the train to come.' Or, 'Lord, keep that light green
until I get there.' And I get all uptight if he does not
answer with what I want. Deep down I still want to
blame him, and that is very foolish and it is a very
wrong attitude towards this loving God. Later I will
explain how I try to deal with this.

The point I am trying to make is how early
impressions of God can penetrate very deep, and if
these impressions are wrong, they can do an immense
amount of damage. Having had to counsel a number
of people, I can say these basic attitudes are quite
common and they can successfully block us from the
truth about God. God has given us a remedy, he has
spoken the truth to us and we must seriously ask

ourselves if we allow our lives to be shaped by these revelations.

Do not be afraid, for I have redeemed you;
I have called you by your name, you are mine.
(Isaiah 43:1)

I shall pour clean water over you and you will be cleansed . . . I shall give you a new heart, and put a new spirit in you.
(Ezekiel 36:25–26)

'It is not the healthy who need the doctor, but the sick. I came to call not the upright, but sinners.'
(Mark 2:17)

'Come to me, all you who labour and are over-burdened, and I will give you rest. Shoulder my yoke and learn from me, for I am gentle and humble in heart, and you will find rest for your souls. Yes, my yoke is easy and my burden light.'
(Matthew 11:28–30)

I found a way out of the problem of wrong images of God through someone who began to explain the story of the Fall for me. As a child, I had accepted the story as it was; it was only much later that I began to question it. I felt a bit hard done by that I, and the rest of humanity, should have to suffer for Adam and Eve's wrong action. It did not seem fair. Later on I grew quite sceptical about the early chapters of Genesis and felt it was a rather naive way to explain the problem of suffering and evil in the world. Because these early chapters seemed irrelevant I did not pay much attention to them.

I can now see that Satan was repeating in me the same strategy that he had used against Adam and Eve. As these chapters were opened to me, I began to see that they were not irrelevant. This was the way Satan still acted today.

Satan set out to undermine Adam and Eve's confidence in God. His plan was to undermine their trust. He starts by asking an innocent question: 'Did God really say you were not to eat from any of the trees in the garden?' Eve replies that it was only from the tree in the middle of the garden that they were forbidden to eat. Here Satan craftily sows doubt. He suggests that God's command, not to eat from the tree of knowledge of good and evil, was because God feared that Adam and Eve would become like him and rival him. Doubt was put into Eve's heart – 'perhaps this God was not so good after all? Perhaps he did not want their growth and development?' It is tragic to think that she was moved to listen to this unknown serpent and take his word rather than the word of the one they knew and with whom they walked.

Satan is in the business of making God look unfavourable and untrustworthy. Ask people what they think about God, and most will have some pretty nasty suspicions about him.

Once I began to see and recognise the wound that the Fall had left in me, I began to see how to deal with Satan. He wanted me to mistrust God, so when God did not grant my every wish, Satan played on that fact, lying to me by saying that God did not love me. The trouble was, I had no firm trust in God; I relied more on what I felt or what I thought.

Today, because I have learnt bad habits, I have to take a firm control of the way I think in times of frustration. It is amazing how when I am in a hurry, things go wrong as though they are out to mess things up. I either lose the keys of the car, or mislay my glasses. The traffic lights change just as I reach them or I get behind a farm tractor and cannot get a chance to over-take. I have to stop myself reacting in my usual way of thinking of God sitting up in heaven waiting to do miracles on demand, but refusing to because he wants to try me out.

Slowly I have come to realise that my pictures of God had come from my feelings or my thoughts. I felt disappointed he did not answer my prayers, so I concluded he was not too interested in me. What I needed was a thorough grounding in what God had said about himself. I have had to take texts from Scripture, texts that tell of the goodness of God and I have had to ponder them, tell him I believe them, and then during the day I have tried to believe them. It has not been easy. Some days are better than others, others are disasters. But, slowly and gradually, I have found some progress has been made.

This is why I see prayer as a dialogue. I like to look at what God has said and then work at trying to believe it. It is not a question of working up one's feelings, or brainstorming, I just repeat the truth and tell God I want to believe it. I thank him for it, and try to live it. I have to admit many failures, but I know I have grown over the years. One day the full effect of his work on Calvary will come to fruition in me. I know I am not able to set myself free, but I also know I have to work along with him who strengthens me.

FOR REFLECTION

1. Is prayer a dialogue for you? If so, who does the speaking first?
2. Do you read the word of God apart from what you hear in church?
3. Would you say there is a difference between Bible study and praying the Scriptures?

4. What do you do when you seem not able to pray?
5. If you find it hard to trust God, try repeating to yourself the Scripture passages printed in this chapter. If necessary, make this a regular thing.

PRAYER

I praise you God that you are not a God of silence. I may not hear your voice, but I have your word and every time I read that I hear you speak. I bless you for all the ways you communicate with me. Lord, keep me wide awake, so that when you come to collect me, I shall be waiting. Amen.

Further copies of Fr. Ian's books

God is Not Angry and **Your Sins are Forgiven**
The God Who Speaks and **You Will Receive Power**
This is My Body and **How Can I Pray ?**

*are available by mail order
from*

Goodnews Books & Audio

**Tel: 01582 571011
Fax: 01582 571012
email: orders@goodnewsbooks.net
www.goodnewsbooks.net**

Send for a Catalogue of Christian Books